Needlework Notebook

Rhiannon Davies
Deputy Headteacher
Aberaeron Comprehensive School

Heinemann Educational Books
London

HEINEMANN EDUCATIONAL BOOKS LTD
London Edinburgh Melbourne Auckland Toronto
Singapore Hong Kong Kuala Lumpur
Ibadan Johannesburg Nairobi
Lusaka New Delhi Kingston

ISBN 0 435 42830 6
© Rhiannon Davies 1968
First published 1968
Reprinted 1969 (twice), 1970, 1972, 1974, 1975
Reprinted with corrections 1977

Published by Heinemann Educational Books Ltd
48 Charles Street, London W1X 8AH
Printed Offset Litho and bound in Great Britain by
Cox & Wyman Ltd, London, Fakenham and Reading

Contents

THE INDIVIDUAL AND HER CLOTHES	1
DRESSMAKING	1
TAKING YOUR MEASUREMENTS	4
USING A SEWING MACHINE	5
STITCHES	7

    Tacking; machine stitching; hemming; slip-hemming; blanket stitch; buttonhole stitch; fish-bone stitch; oversewing; whipping; herringbone stitch; overcasting; back-stitching; hem stitch; faggotting; herringbone stitch; chain stitch; satin stitch; stem stitch; feather stitch; cross stitch

SEAMS	14

    Open seam; run and fell seam; flat-stitched seam; french seam; mantua seam; flannel seam I; flannel seam II

EDGES	22

    Hems; bias binding and crossway strips; bindings; facings; french binding; flannel binding; piping; shell hemming; rouleau strips; methods of attaching lace

OPENINGS	34

    Continuous openings; faced openings; bound openings; wrap and facing openings

FASTENINGS	39

    Buttons; worked buttonholes; bound buttonholes; worked loops; rouleau loops; zip fasteners; hooks and eyes; press studs; tapes; eyelet holes; faced slots; unstiffened belts; belt loops

FULLNESS	51

    Inverted pleats; box pleats; tucks; flares; gores; gathering; gauging; smocking; yokes

SETTING A CUFF ON A LONG SLEEVE	56
SETTING ON A COLLAR	57
SETTING IN A SLEEVE	58
SETTING A WAISTBAND ON A SKIRT	60
POCKETS	61

ARROWHEADS   62

DARNING   63
Thin place darns; darning a hole; darning a hole in a knitted fabric; diagonal cut darn; hedge tear darn; Swiss darning; machine darning

PATCHING   70
A mitred corner; calico patch (by hand); calico patch (by machine); woollen patch; print patch

FIBRES AND FABRICS   76
Wool; silk; cotton; linen; rayon viscose; rayon acetate; nylon; Orlon; Terylene; Dynel

FABRIC MIXTURES   84

IDENTIFICATION OF FIBRES   85

INTERLINING   86

HANDLING DIFFICULT FABRICS   87
Velvet and corduroy; lace; plastics (P.V.C.); Courtelle jersey; fur fabrics

GENERAL RULES FOR PRESSING   89

STAIN REMOVAL   91

The individual and her clothes

1 Know yourself—your good points and your bad points.
2 Select a design that is flattering to your figure as well as to your personality.
3 Choose a fabric that is flattering to you in colour, texture and weight, and that is suitable for the pattern chosen.
4 Choose accessories carefully according to your age, type of figure, style of garment and the occasion for which it was designed. Your clothes and accessories should look as if they are going to the same place.
5 Remember personal grooming. Correct posture, grace and a pleasant manner are very important.
6 Store your clothes according to type of garment and fabric. Many fabrics are inclined to stretch and therefore these should either be folded and stored or else hung very carefully.
7 Take your clothes out of the wardrobe or storage in good time and hang up so that any creases will hang out.
8 Keep your clothes, including undergarments, in good repair. Replace a button and mend a tear immediately.
9 Keep all your clothes fresh and clean. Do not store away dirty garments—wash them if they are washable and send the rest to the dry-cleaners regularly.

Dressmaking

To ensure success in dressmaking, it is essential to use a good pattern and the right fabric for the design.

Accuracy is vital at every stage; a professional-looking garment cannot be achieved without it.

Select your sewing time carefully. If you can spend only short periods at any one time, plan your work so that something is accomplished in each period. Allow sufficient time for each stage. Do not rush your sewing or sew when it is time to see to some other responsibility; this will only make you impatient and dissatisfied with the result.

Choosing a Pattern:
1 Decide exactly what is needed. If you have decided to make a simple cotton

dress, resist the temptation to buy a pattern for a dainty chiffon dress or you will be disappointed with the result.
2. When you have found a pattern that appeals to you, consider carefully whether or not this design suits your type of figure.
3. Buy the pattern by the correct bust size. It is easier to adjust the skirt or alter the length of the bodice than it is to make the bodice wider. Beginners should have as little adjusting as possible.

Choosing Material:

1. Study the pattern envelope for the list of suggested fabrics and the length required.
2. Be careful to buy a fabric that is suitable for the style that you have chosen. Avoid fabrics with a pile, such as velvet or corduroy, and one-way printed designs unless the pattern is intended for them.
3. Avoid a fabric that frays and loosely woven fabrics because these are inclined to get out of shape and shrink.

Cutting out:

1. Collect everything together – pins, needles, tacking cotton, cutting-out scissors, tape-measure, tailor's chalk, thimble, fabric and pattern.
2. Sort out the pattern and return all unwanted pieces to the envelope.
3. Check the fit. Pin front to back and make all necessary adjustments.
4. Press out all creases from the fabric and fold as required. Woollen fabrics, tapes and zips should be shrunk before use unless marked 'pre-shrunk'.
5. Never cut out on a small surface – choose a large table or a clean floor.
6. Follow carefully the diagrams on the instruction sheet for laying pattern pieces on the fabric. These have been worked out by experts with special regard to the use of the grain of the fabric.
7. Check on seam and hem allowances. Most reliable patterns allow for seam turnings and hems so that you may cut close to the paper pattern. If by any chance this is not so, a margin must be allowed and the usual allowances are $\frac{1}{2}'' - \frac{5}{8}''$ (1·5 cm.) for all seams and $2\frac{1}{4}''$ (6 cm.) for hems.
8. Each pattern piece carries a series of perforations or markings (see page 3) which are very important in the cutting out and in the assembling of the various parts.
9. Pin in position, taking care that the paper pattern is flat on the fabric.
10. Cut around leaving folded edges as they are.
11. Mark with chalk or tailor's tacking all balance marks and seam allowances before removing the paper pattern.

12 Follow carefully the instructions given on the instruction sheet and press as you sew. Accuracy pays. A professional looking garment is the result of measuring, marking and stitching accurately.
13 Use interlining for a better finish on all collars, cuffs, lapels etc.
14 All seams and pleats should be sewn from the bottom to the top and from the outside of the shoulder to the neckline.
15 Always pay particular attention to the finish of a garment. The inside is just as important as the outside.

PATTERN MARKINGS

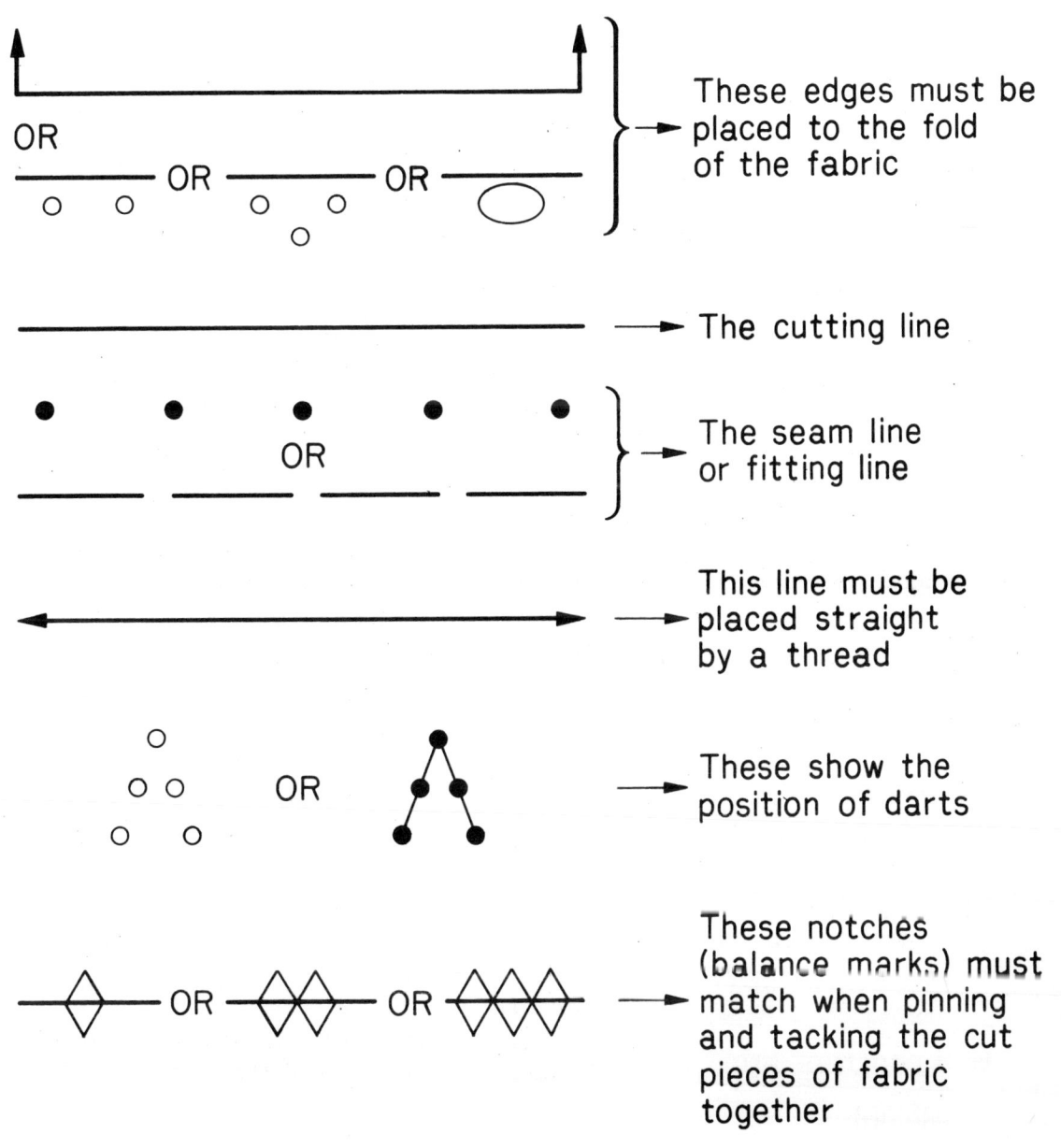

These edges must be placed to the fold of the fabric

The cutting line

The seam line or fitting line

This line must be placed straight by a thread

These show the position of darts

These notches (balance marks) must match when pinning and tacking the cut pieces of fabric together

"Misses" sizes in paper patterns.

Size	Bust	Waist	Hip	Nape → Waist
10	32½" (83 cm)	25" (64 cm)	34½" (88 cm)	16" (40 cm)
12	34" (86 cm)	26½" (67 cm)	36" (91 cm)	16¼" (40.5 cm)
14	36" (91 cm)	28" (71 cm)	38" (97 cm)	16½" (41 cm)
16	38" (97 cm)	30" (76 cm)	40" (102 cm)	16¾" (42 cm)

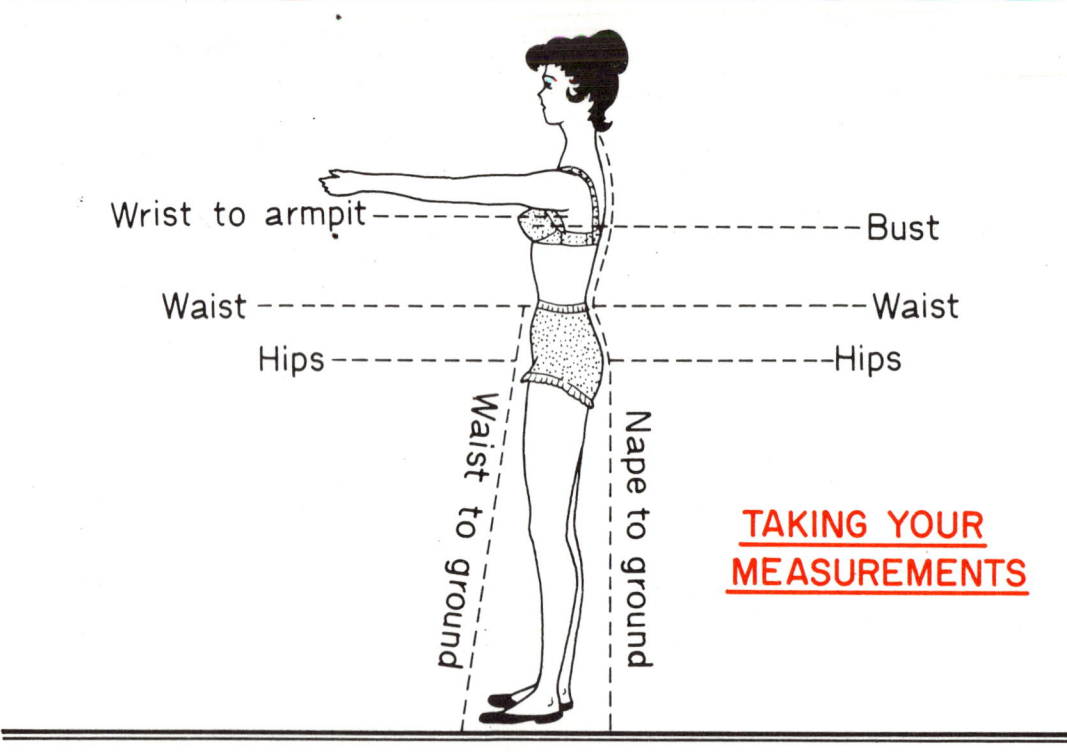

Wrist to armpit ---------- Bust
Waist ---------- Waist
Hips ---------- Hips

Waist to ground

Nape to ground

TAKING YOUR MEASUREMENTS

PERSONAL MEASUREMENTS

	1st. Yr	2nd. Yr	3rd. Yr	4th. Yr	5th. Yr
1. Bust =					
2. Waist =					
3. Hips (7" (18 cm) below waist) =					
4. Length of back (nape of neck → waist) =					
5. Length of skirt (waist → hem) =					
6. Length of arm =					
7. Height =					

THE METRIC SYSTEM

10 millimetres (mm) = 1 centimetre (cm)
10 centimetres = 1 decimetre (dm)
10 decimetres = 1 metre (m)
1 metre = 39·37 inches   0·9144 m = 1 yard

Approximate equivalents

$\frac{3}{8}''$ = 1 cm	18" or $\frac{1}{2}$ yd	= 45 cm or 0·45 m
$\frac{1}{2}''$ = 1·25 cm	27" or $\frac{3}{4}$ yd	= 70 cm or 0·7 m
$\frac{5}{8}''$ = 1·5 cm	36" or 1 yd	= 91 cm or 0·91 m
1" = 2·5 cm	45" or $1\frac{1}{4}$ yd	= 115 cm or 1·15 m
$2\frac{1}{4}''$ = 5·75 cm	54" or $1\frac{1}{2}$ yd	= 140 cm or 1·4 m

Using a sewing machine

A good and reliable sewing machine is practically indispensable to the dressmaker. It is, therefore, important to understand how to handle it with care and keep it in good working order. Always read the handbook carefully then:

1. See that the machine is free from dust and fluff.
2. Oil it regularly, but be sure that all surplus oil is wiped away before using.
3. Use the correct sized needle according to the fabric being sewn, and see that it is inserted correctly.
4. Use the correct thread on the reel and in the bobbin. Fine work – fine thread – fine needle. Use cotton on cotton fabrics, silk on silk and wool, and synthetic thread on synthetic fabrics.
5. Wind the bobbin and set it in position, allowing a length of thread free at the end.
6. Thread the needle according to the machine in use. Holding the free end of the thread from the needle with the left hand, turn the wheel towards the worker once so that the needle goes down once and comes up again. This should bring up the bobbin thread. Both threads should then be pushed towards the back with the 'thread take-up lever' at the top.
7. The stitch-regulator should then be adjusted according to the number of stitches required per inch, and the tension tested on a piece of double fabric similar to the one to be sewn.
8. Lower the needle carefully so that it pierces the fabric at the starting point, lower the presser foot gently and begin to sew.
9. Never pull or push the fabric as it is being sewn – guide it.

10 Before removing fabric, lift lever for presser-foot, seeing that the 'thread take-up lever' is up. Draw the fabric to the back and cut both threads together.
11 Finish off neatly on W.S.
12 The automatic swing needle machine may be adjusted for use in neatening raw edges, darning, sewing buttons, working buttonholes and embroidery.

Fault Finding:

1 Thread Breaking: needle may be set incorrectly, or it may be bent or blunt. Tension may be too tight. Machine may be threaded incorrectly.
2 Missing Stitches: needle may be too fine for the thread used, or needle not accurately set, or needle bent or blunt.
3 Stitches Looping: incorrect threading, or either top or bottom tension is too loose.
4 Fabric Puckering: needle may be too coarse, or stitches may be too long, especially if sewing on fine fabric. Tensions may be too tight.

THREAD AND MACHINE NEEDLE CHART

Size of Needle			
English	Continental	Fabrics	Size of Thread
9	70	Lightweight and delicate fabrics, muslin, silk and cambric	100–150 cotton 30 silk
11	80	Silk, fine linens, shirtings, calico, poplin, lawn	80–100 cotton 24–30 silk
14	90	General work, shirtings, sheeting calico, domestic goods	60–80 cotton 20 silk
16	100	Light woollen fabrics, heavy calico drill	40–60 cotton 16–18 silk
18	110	Woollen materials, ticking, trousers, boys' clothing	30–40 cotton 10–12 silk
19	120	Heavy woollens, coats, bags, heavy clothing, ticking, trousers	24–30 cotton 60–80 linen
21	130	Coarse cloth, bags, heavy material of any texture	40–60 linen very coarse cotton

Use synthetic thread for all rayons and synthetic fabrics. The size of the needle used depends upon the weight of the fabric.

Stitches

Temporary Stitches:
1 Even Tacking: Used for holding parts of garment firmly in place so that the permanent stitches may be worked accurately.
2 Long and Short Tacking: Used on single fabric for marking-out purposes.
3 Tailor's Tacking: Used on double thickness of fabric for marking-out purposes.
4 Diagonal Tacking or Basting: Used for holding a pleat in position.

Permanent Stitches:
1 Stitches used for neatening raw edges:
    Blanket stitch
    Overcasting
    Buttonhole stitch
    Herringbone stitch
2 Stitches used for controlling fullness:
    Running stitch
    Gathering
3 Stitches used to hold different parts of the garment together:
    Machine stitch
    Back stitch
    Oversewing
4 Decorative stitches also used in the construction of the garment:
    Hem-stitching
    Faggoting
    Saddle-stitching
5 Embroidery stitches:
    Feather-stitch
    Cross-stitch etc.

TEMPORARY STITCHES

EVEN TACKING.

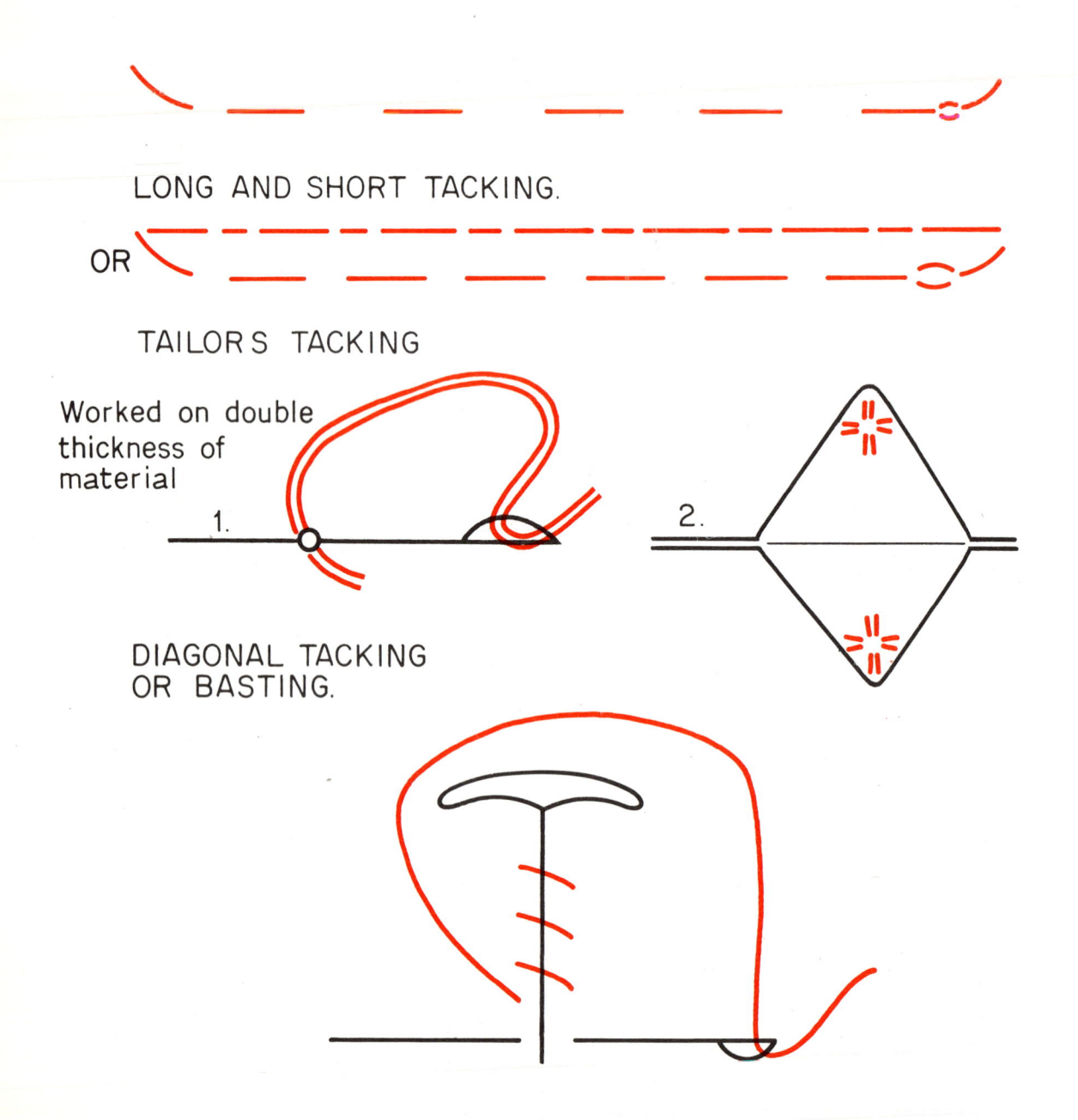

LONG AND SHORT TACKING.

OR

TAILORS TACKING

Worked on double thickness of material

1.

2.

DIAGONAL TACKING OR BASTING.

PERMANENT STITCHES

MACHINE-STITCH.

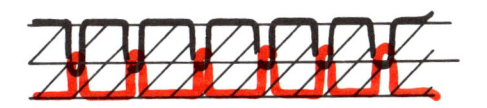

Needle thread
Double thickness of fabric
Bobbin thread

Needle and bobbin threads pull evenly and balance correctly.

Incorrect tension

1. Needle thread too tight and it lies in a straight line along fabric.

To remedy: Loosen tension screw which controls spring above needle. If it persists, tighten screw on bobbin case.

2. Bobbin thread too tight and it lies in a straight line along fabric.

To remedy: Tighten tension screw which controls spring above needle. If it persists, loosen screw on bobbin case.

HEMMING. R to L

SLIP-HEMMING. R to L

BLANKET OR LOOP STITCH
L to R

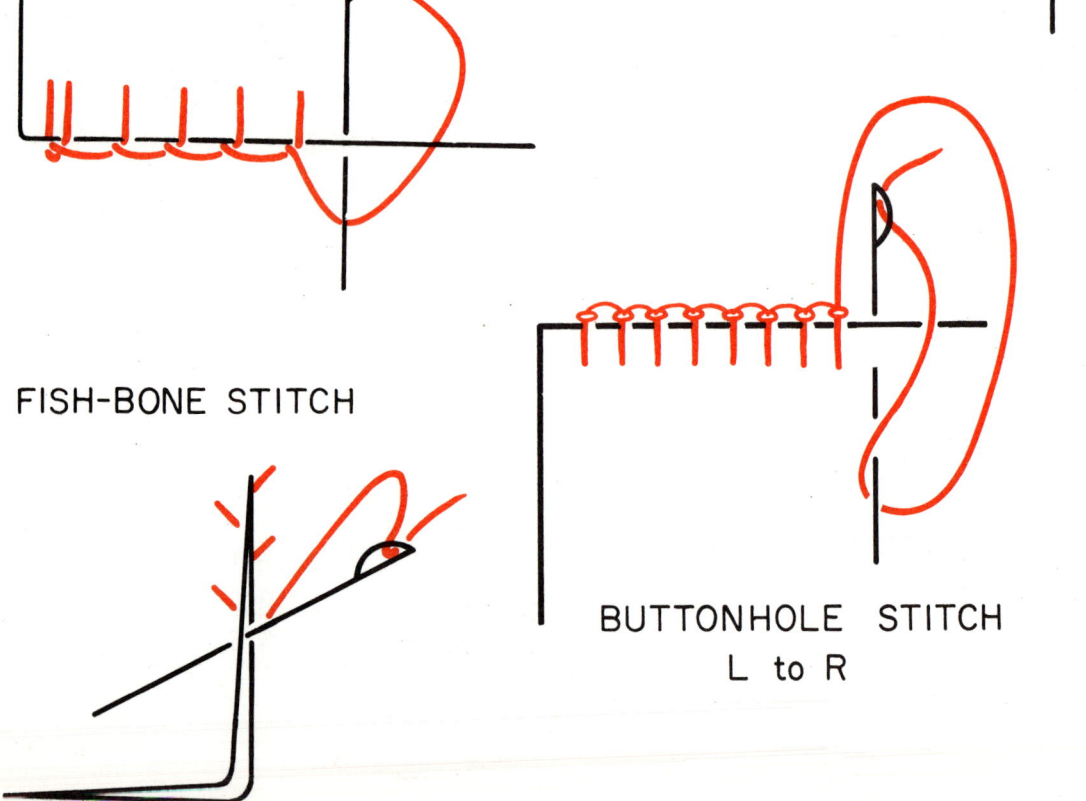

FISH-BONE STITCH

BUTTONHOLE STITCH
L to R

OVERSEWING (or sewing) R to L

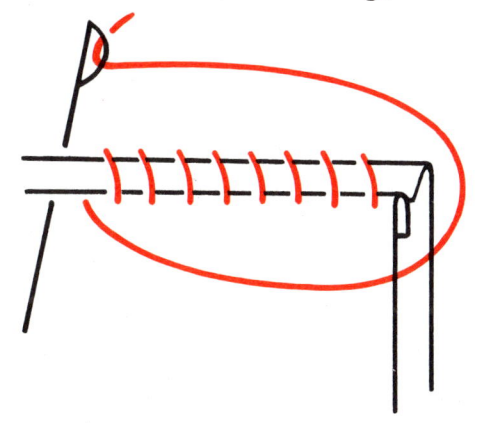

WHIPPING (a rolled hem)

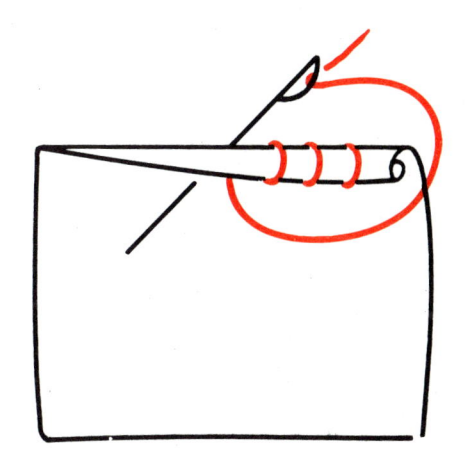

HERRINGBONE STITCH L to R

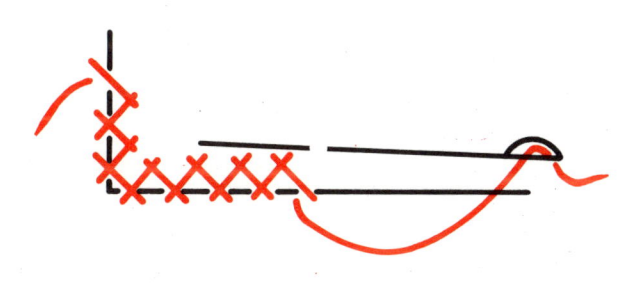

OVERCASTING L to R

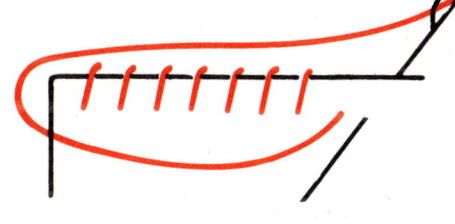

BACK-STITCHING R to L

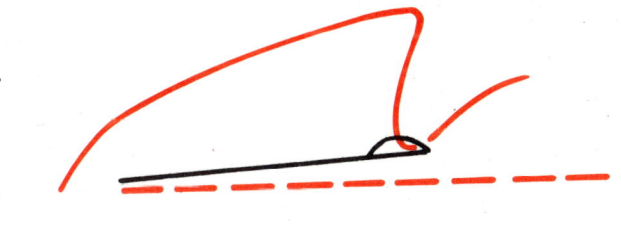

STITCHING R to L

HEM STITCH R to L or L to R

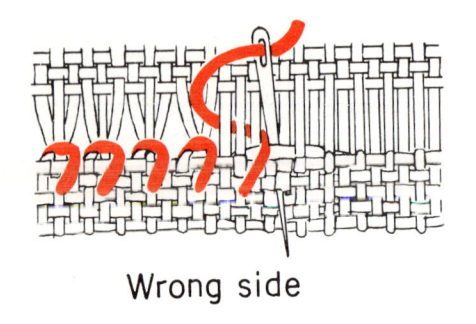

Wrong side

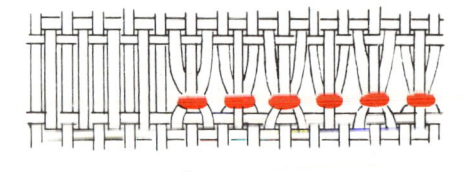

Right side

FAGGOTING

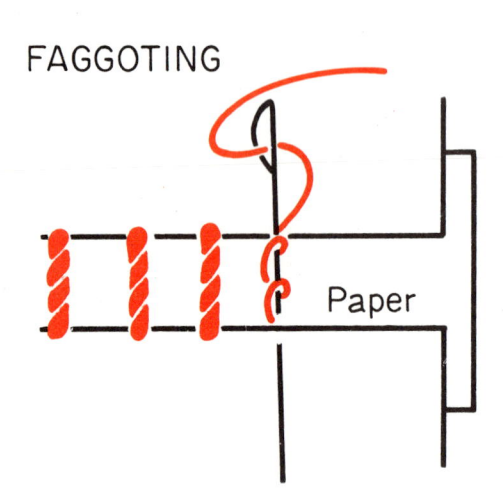

Paper

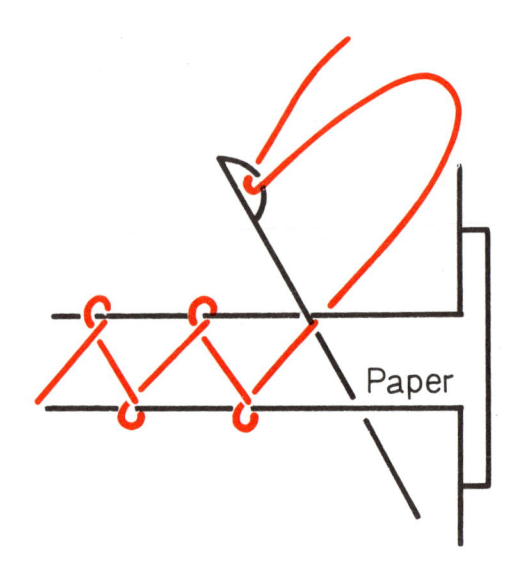

Paper

HERRINGBONE STITCH (used closely for shadow work on sheer fabrics)

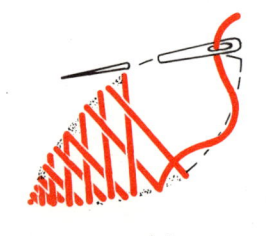

Wrong side

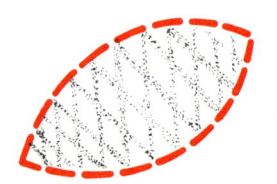

Right side

CHAIN STITCH.

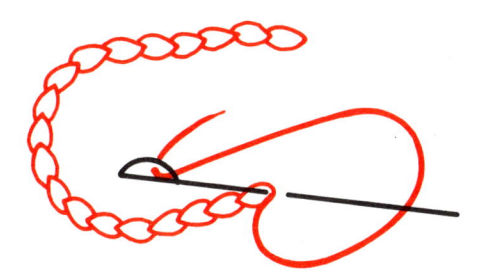

SATIN STITCH

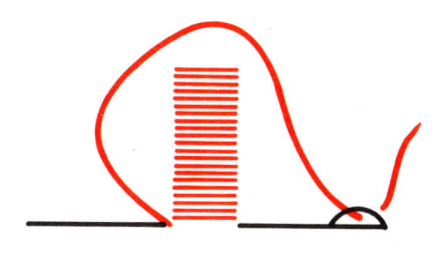

STEM STITCH

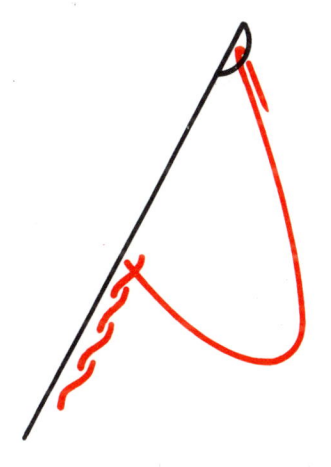

FEATHER STITCH

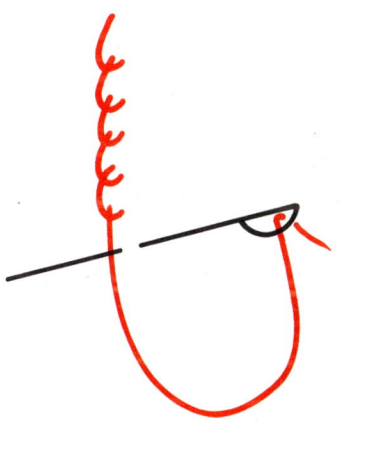

CROSS STITCH

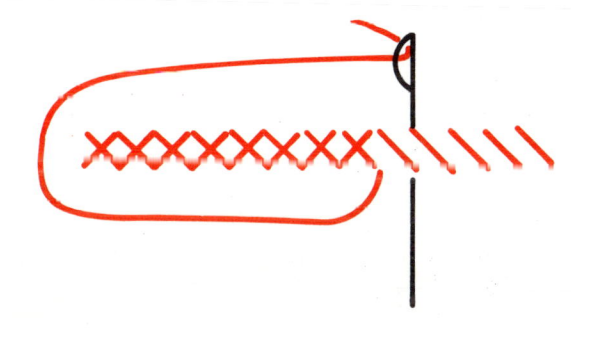

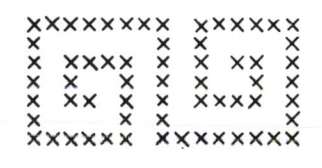

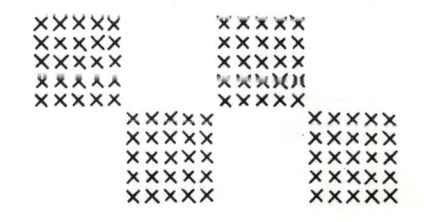

Seams

Choice of seams depends upon:
1 Effect required on R.S.
2 Fabric used

Seams may be divided into 3 classes:
1 Flat Seams:
    Run and Fell seam
    Counter Hem seam
    Open seam
    Machine stitched seam
    Linked seam (using faggoting)
2 Ridged Seams:
    French seam
    Mantua maker seam
3 Flannel seams.

OPEN SEAM

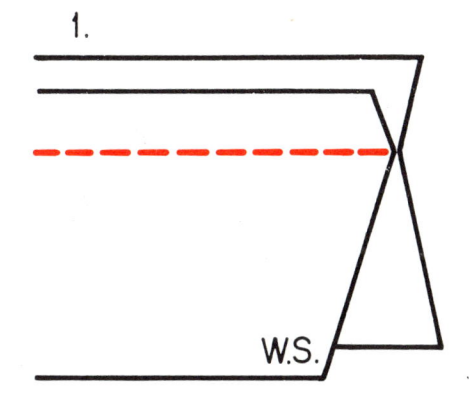

1.

Tack and machine stitch along fitting line on W.S.

2.

Remove tackings. Press seam open. Trim raw edges and neaten.

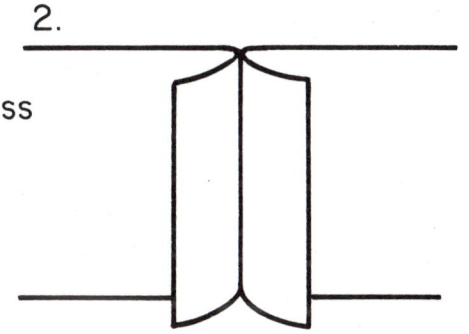

<u>Use</u>: *On most outer garments, skirts, dresses, slacks, etc.*

METHODS OF NEATENING RAW EDGES.

By means of a machine-made edge-stitch, or by one of the following methods,—

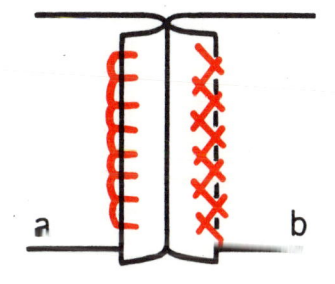

a. Blanket stitch

b. Herringbone stitch

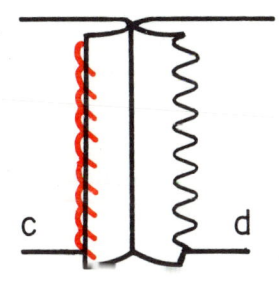

c. Overcasting
   (against the grain of the fabric)

d. Pinking

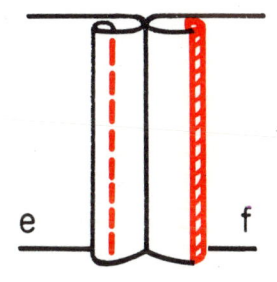

e. Machined fold

f. Binding

RUN AND FELL SEAM

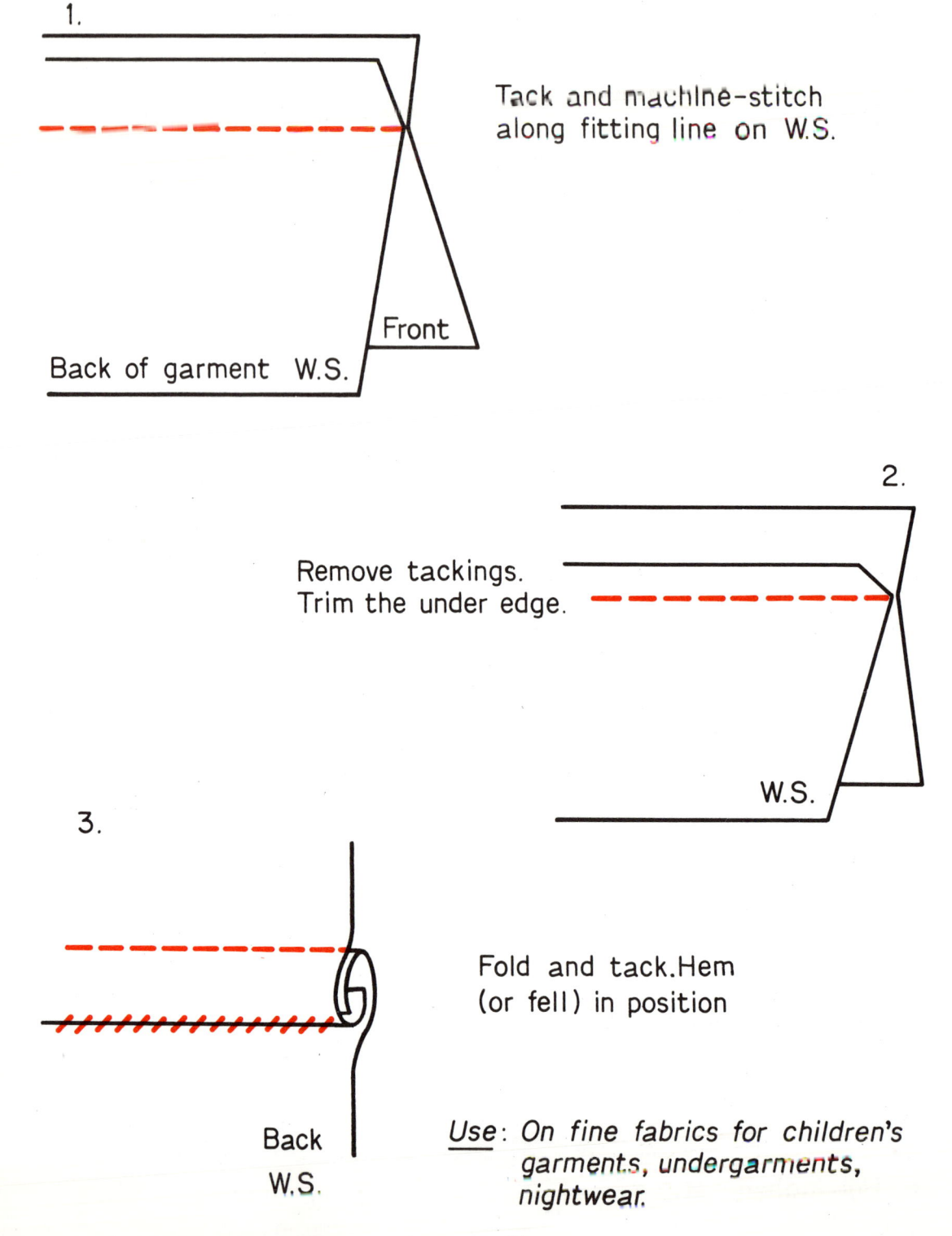

1.

Tack and machine-stitch along fitting line on W.S.

Back of garment W.S. Front

2.

Remove tackings.
Trim the under edge.

W.S.

3.

Fold and tack. Hem (or fell) in position

Back W.S.

Use: On fine fabrics for children's garments, undergarments, nightwear.

16

FLAT STITCHED SEAM
OR
MACHINE-STITCHED SEAM

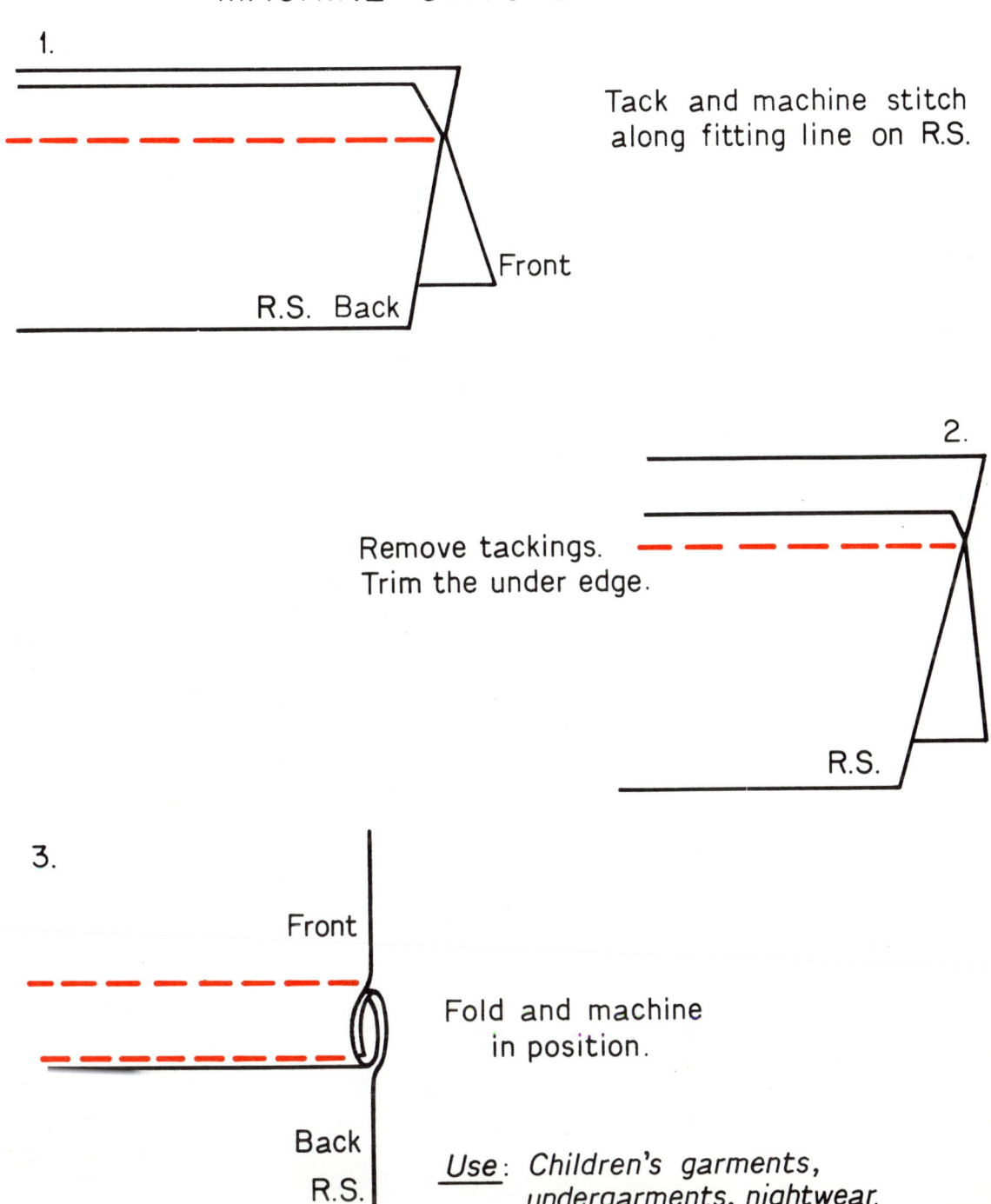

1.

Tack and machine stitch along fitting line on R.S.

Front
R.S. Back

2.

Remove tackings.
Trim the under edge.

R.S.

3.

Front

Fold and machine in position.

Back
R.S.

<u>Use</u>: *Children's garments, undergarments, nightwear.*

17

FRENCH SEAM

1. Tack and machine stitch $\frac{1}{4}"$ (·5cm) above fitting line.

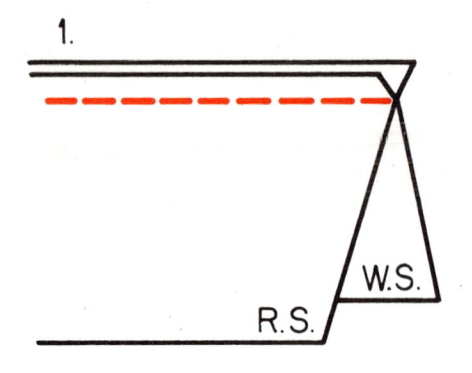

2. Remove tackings. Press seam open on R.S. Trim the edges to 3mm.

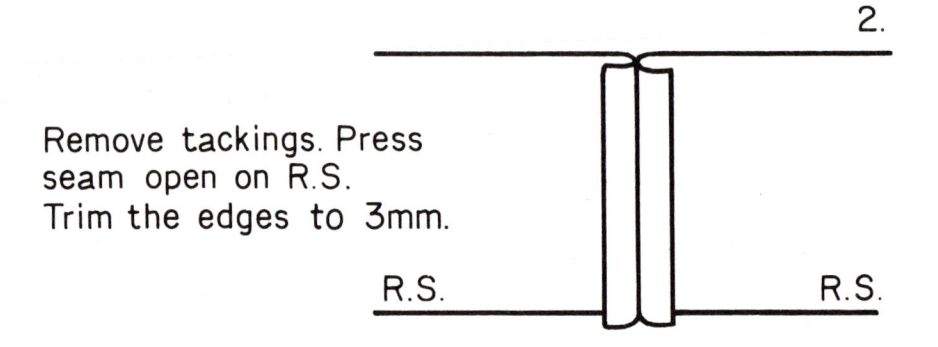

3. Tack and machine-stitch along fitting line to enclose all previous turnings.

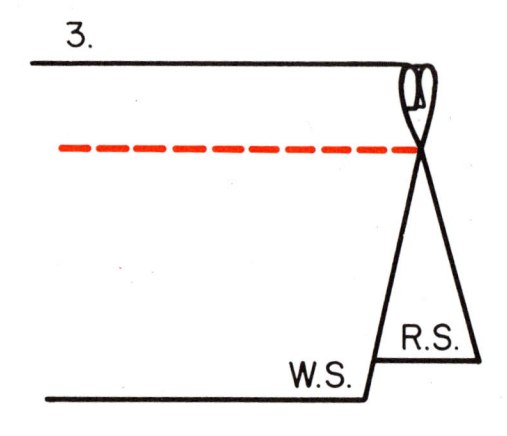

Use: On fabrics which are not thick and bulky for dresses, blouses and cotton garments

MANTUA SEAM

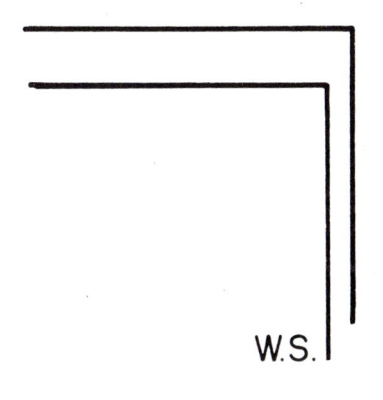

Trim away about ¼" (·5cm) from one edge.

W.S.

Fold over and tack ¼" (·5cm) above fitting line

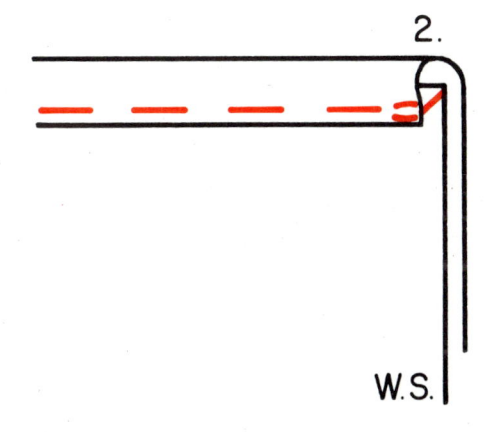

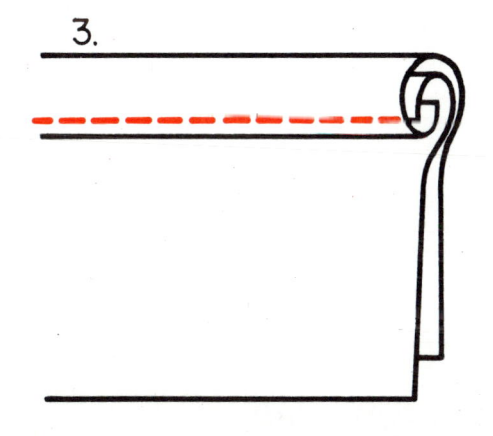

2.

W.S.

3.

Fold over again, tack and machine-stitch through fold and along fitting line

<u>Use</u>: On fine fabrics or for heavywear such as overalls

FLANNEL SEAM I

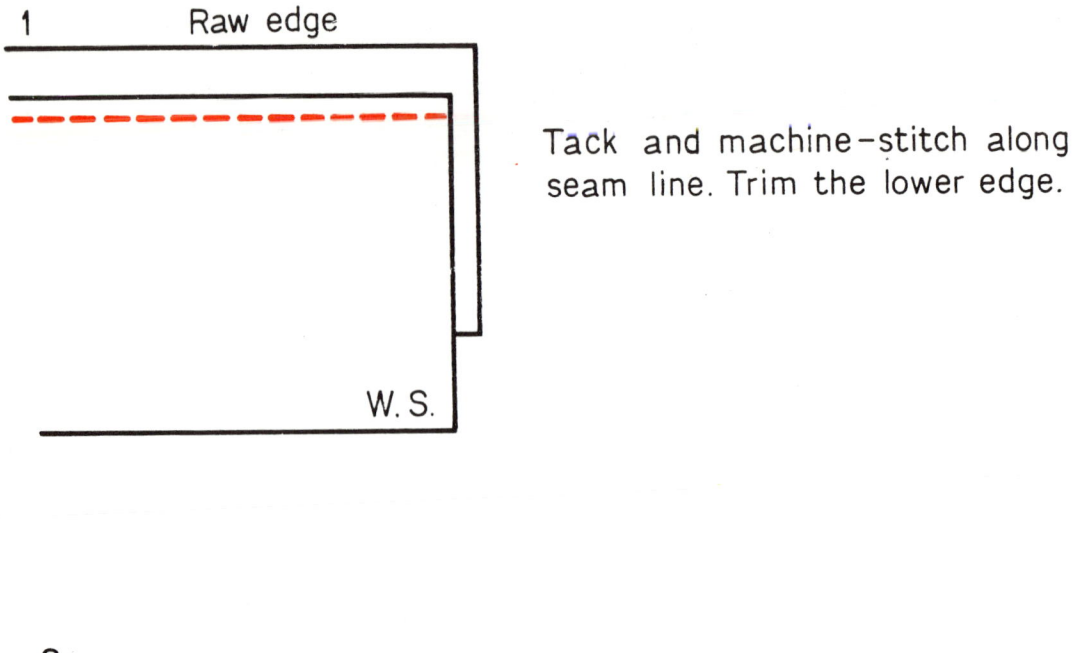

1.

Tack and machine-stitch along seam line. Trim the lower edge.

W.S.

2.

Tack upper raw edge down in position and herringbone-stitch.

W.S.

Use: On flannel and all bulky fabrics where double folds would be thick and clumsy.

FLANNEL SEAM II

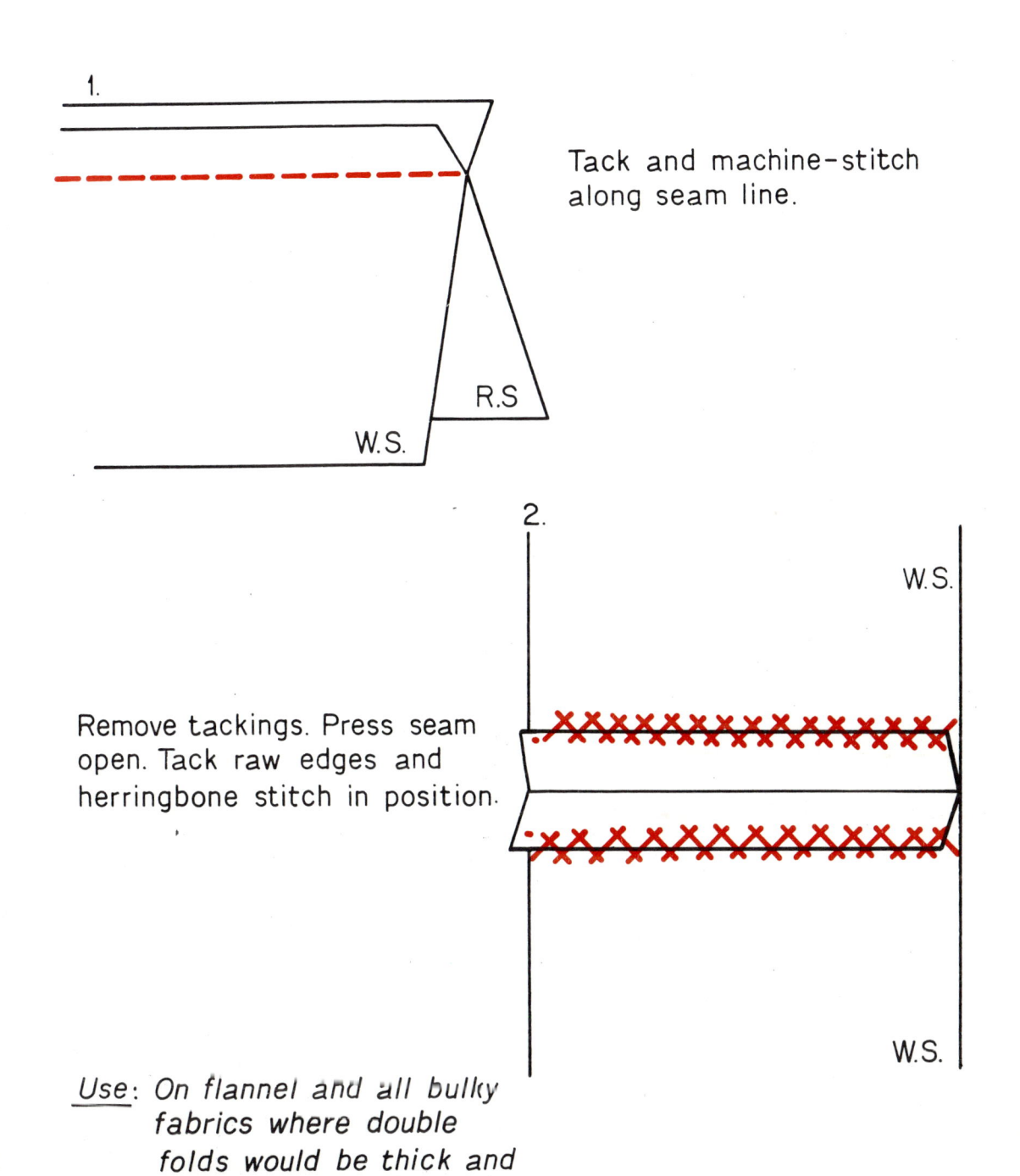

1.

Tack and machine-stitch along seam line.

R.S
W.S.

2.

W.S.

Remove tackings. Press seam open. Tack raw edges and herringbone stitch in position.

W.S.

<u>Use</u>: On flannel and all bulky fabrics where double folds would be thick and clumsy.

Edges

Facts to consider:
1 Fabric – design and texture
2 Style of garment
3 Shape of edge
4 Number of seams merging into edge
5 Finished effect required

Self neatening edges:
1 Hems
2 French binding
3 Embroidery (e.g. scalloped edge finished with loop stitch)

Application of self or contrasting fabric:
1 Binding
2 Facing
3 Piping
4 Rouleau Strips
5 Frilling
6 Flouncing
7 Ruching
8 Braiding
9 Lace or Net

```
        A HEM                      A FOLD
```

A hem may be held in position by means of, —

    1. Hemming
    2. Slip-hemming
    3. Rows of machine-stitching
    4. Hem-stitching
    5. Whipping (if hem is narrow)
    6. Paris binding or bias strips used on a single fold
    7. Herringbone stitch used on a single fold
    8. Slip-hemming with a machined fold
    9. Shell-hemming

A garment may be lengthened by, —

    1. Adding a false hem.
    2. Adding a frill, flounce, lace or ruche.
    3. Faggoting a rouleau strip.
    4. Adding a wide binding.
    5. An insertion.

BIAS BINDING AND CROSS-WAY STRIPS

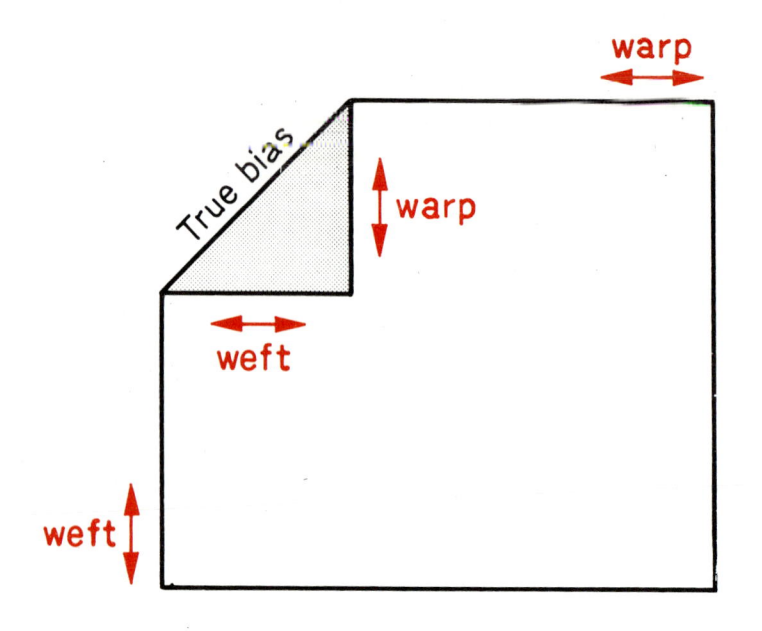

JOINING OF BIAS BINDING

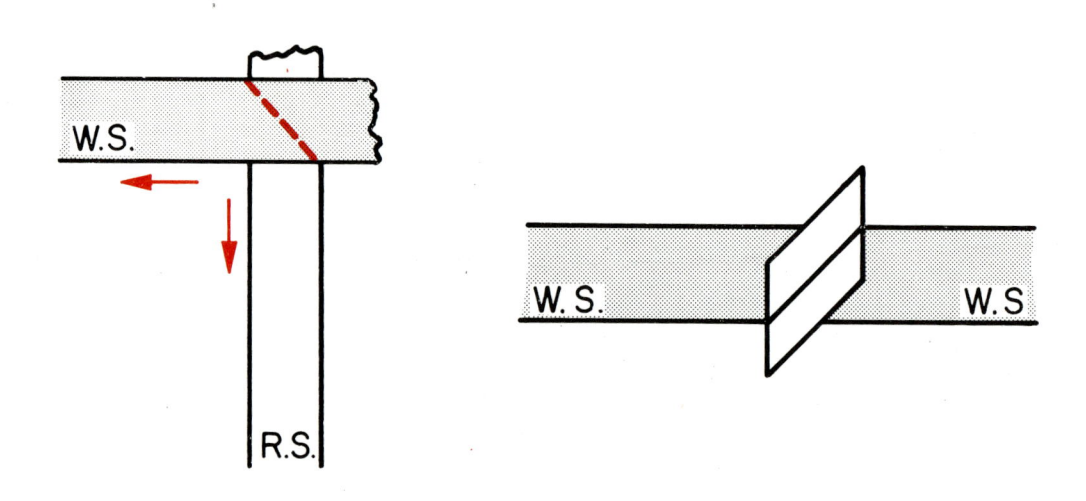

BINDINGS

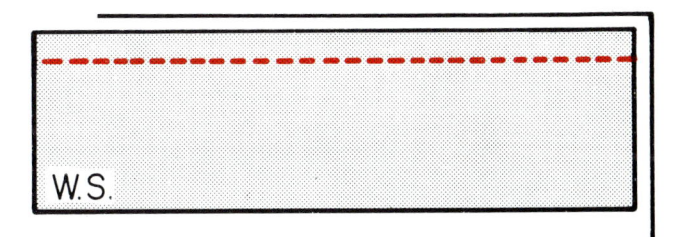

Crease the binding lengthwise into 4 equal parts. With right sides together, tack and machine-stitch binding to the edge along the first crease. Snip all curved edges.

N.B. Binding should be stretched on all concave curves and eased along all convex curves.

2.

Remove tackings. Fold binding along third crease and hem in position on W.S., picking up stitches which come through from R.S.

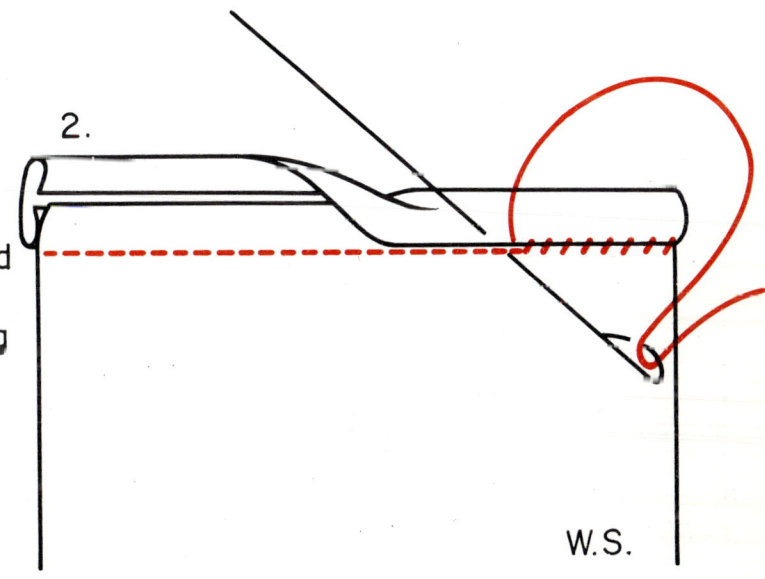

FACING

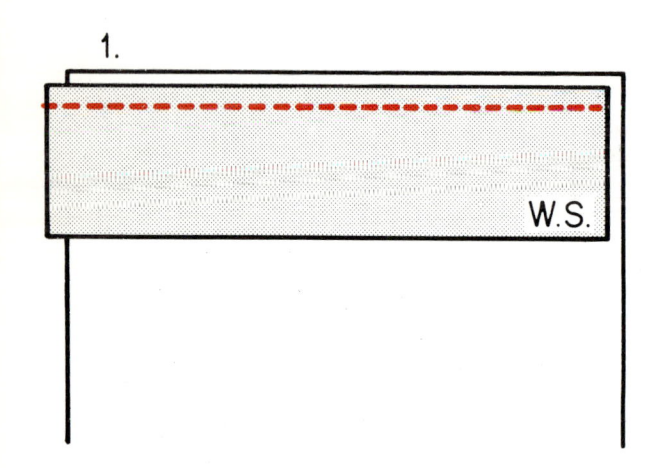

1.

W.S.

Tack and machine-stitch facing onto R.S. or W.S. of garment. Snip all curved edges.

2a

R.S.

Remove tackings. Turn a fold and machine-stitch in position on R.S. so that the facing cannot be seen from W.S.

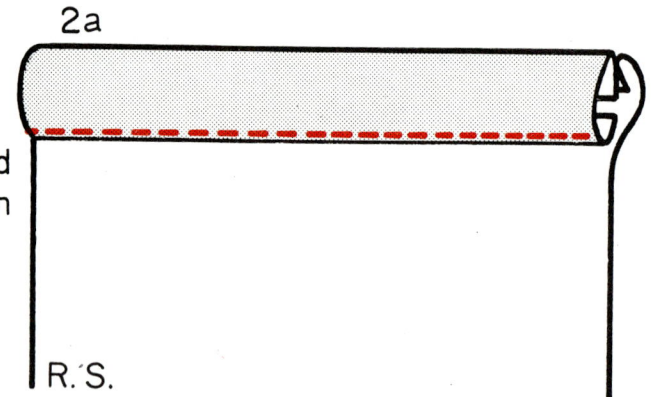

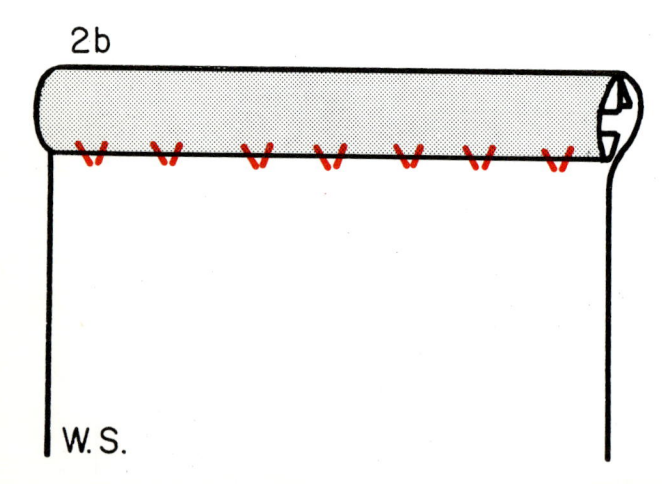

2b

W.S.

Remove tackings. Turn a fold and slip-hem in position on W.S. so that facing cannot be seen from R.S.

ARMHOLE FACING OR NECK FACING

1. Join all seams. Press and neaten.

2. With right sides facing, stitch facing to edge. Trim away surplus material and snip the edges

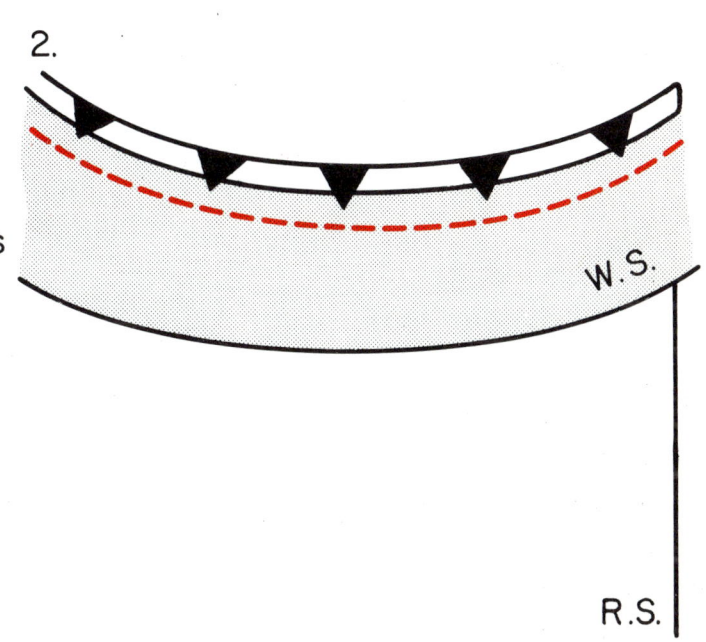

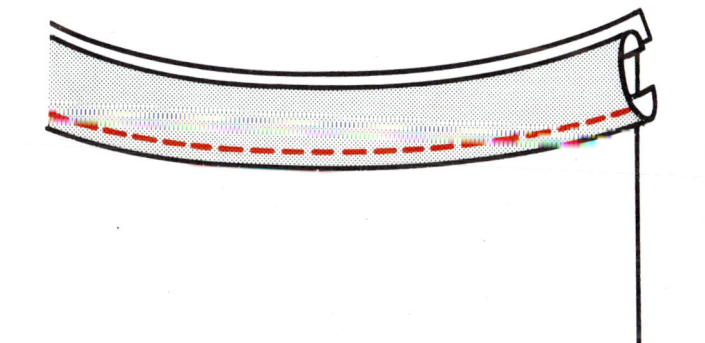

W.S.

R.S.

Turn facing to inside of garment. Press. Turn a fold along raw edge and stitch, keeping it free from garment. Catch-stitch the facing to every seam

W.S.

FRENCH BINDING
OR
IMITATION BINDING

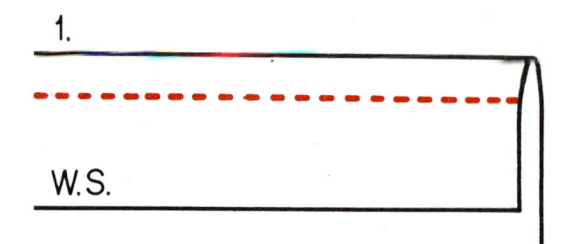

1.

W.S.

R.S.

Turn a fold, width of which should = four times the width of required binding. Crease the fold lengthwise into 4 equal parts. Tack and machine-stitch along first crease.

2.

Remove tackings. Turn binding over to W.S. Turn in fold along 3rd crease and hem in position by picking up stitches which appear through from R.S.

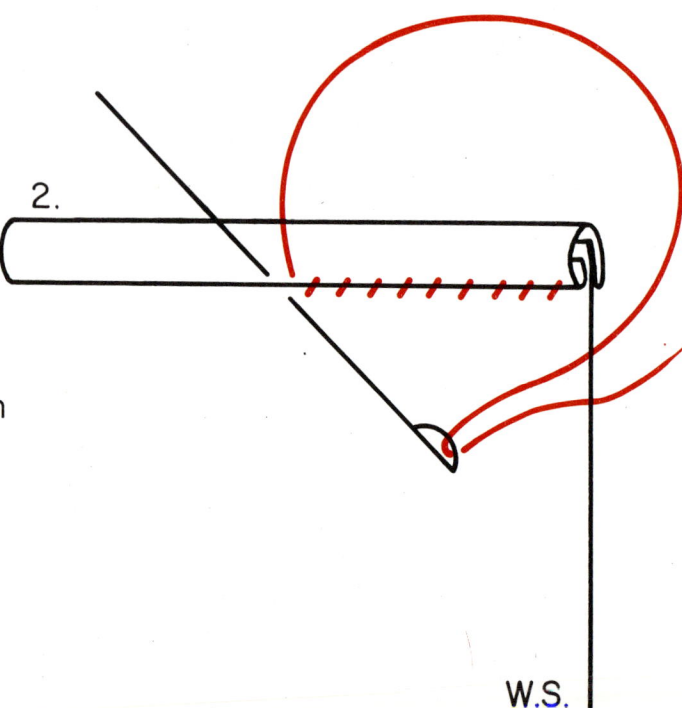

W.S.

FLANNEL BINDING

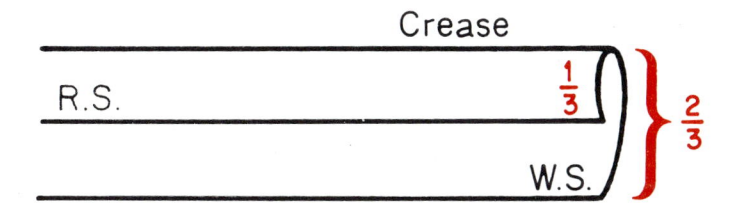

Flannel may be bound with ribbon, silk or french tape. Binding is creased at a depth of $\frac{1}{3}$ width from R. to W.S.

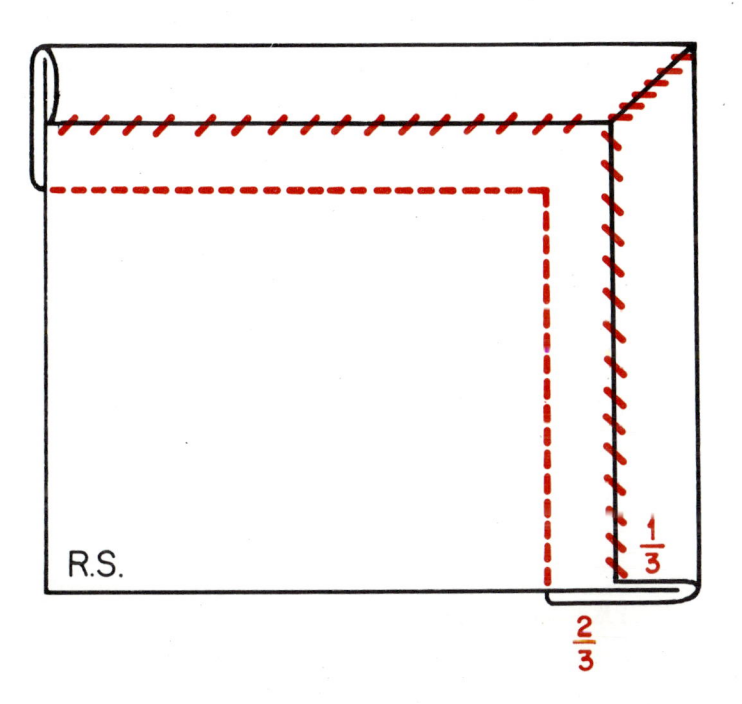

Hemming (felling) on R.S. and W.S.

or

Hemming on R.S. and running stitch on W.S.

PIPED EDGE

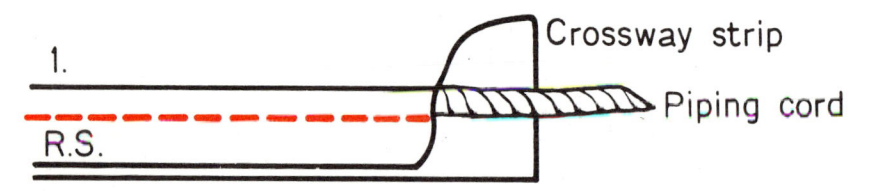

1. Crossway strip / Piping cord / R.S.

N.B. Always wash cord before use because it shrinks.
The cord is secured within the cross-way strip of material by means of running stitches or machine-stitching.

Piping cord tacked in position on R.S. of garment.

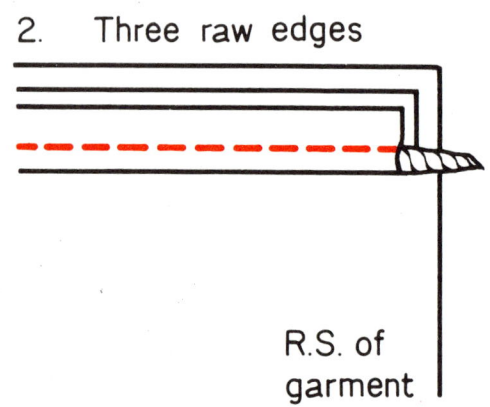

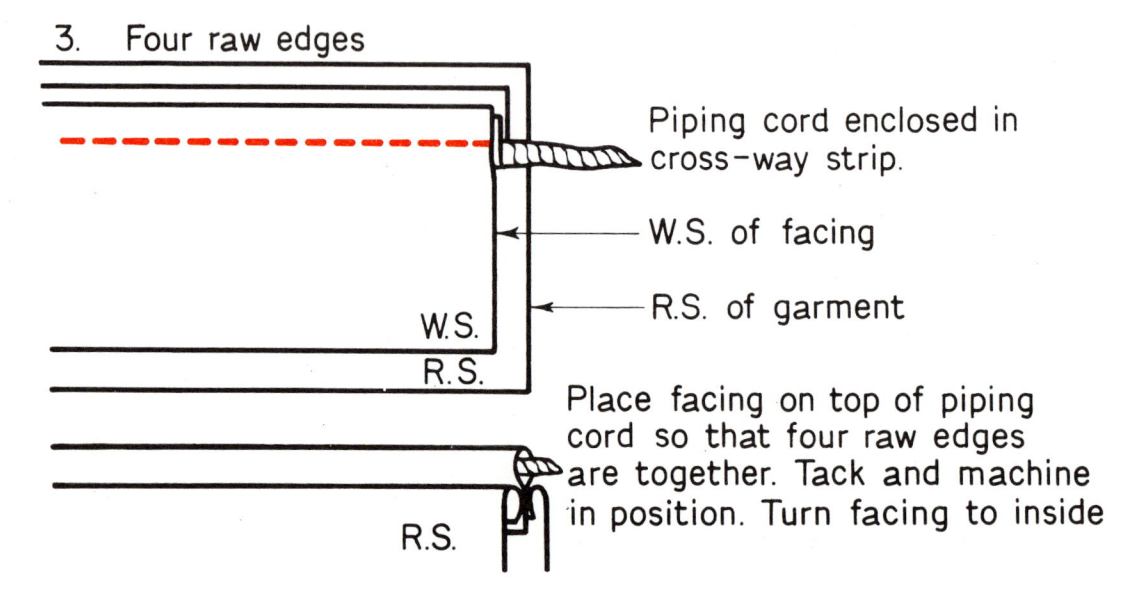

2. Three raw edges

R.S. of garment

3. Four raw edges

Piping cord enclosed in cross-way strip.

W.S. of facing

R.S. of garment

Place facing on top of piping cord so that four raw edges are together. Tack and machine in position. Turn facing to inside

SHELL - HEMMING

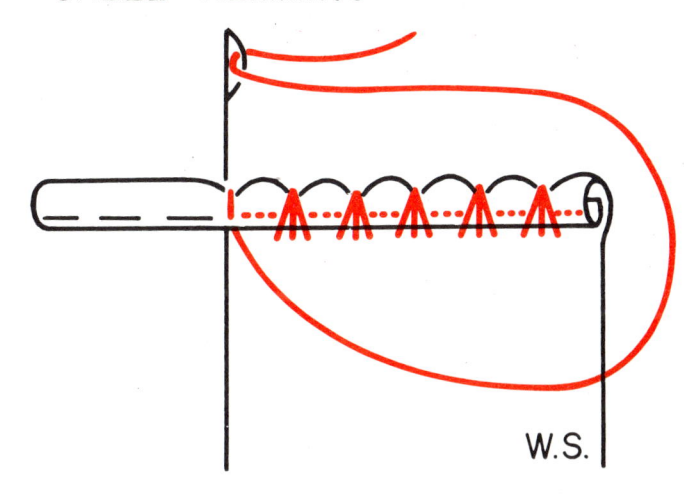

Narrow hem turned and tacked. Hem secured by means of three running-stitches and three over-stitches work alternately.

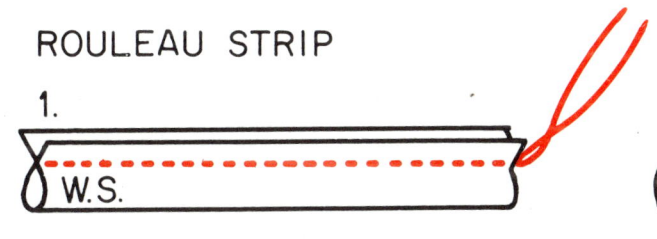

W.S.

ROULEAU STRIP

1.

W.S.

Machine-stitch, stretching the material as it is being sewn.

2.

R.S.

Sew a bodkin firmly to one end of the rouleau and turn the strip right side out over the bodkin.

Rouleau strip
Paper
Garment

R.S.

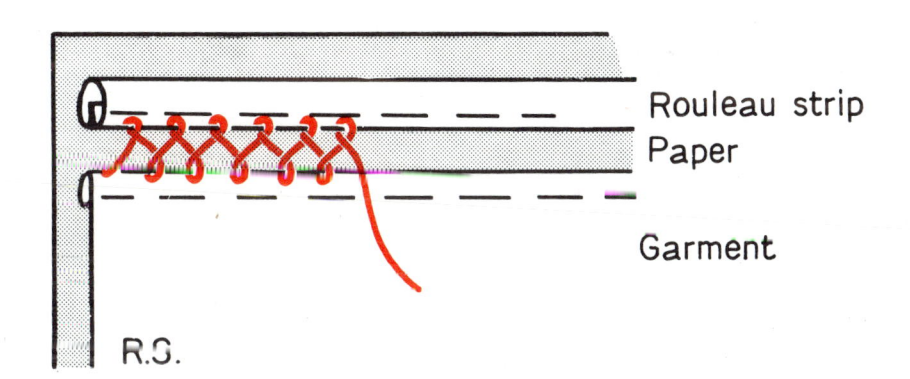

The rouleau strip may be attached to the garment by means of faggoting or insertion stitch or buttonhole stitch

METHODS OF ATTACHING LACE TO A GARMENT

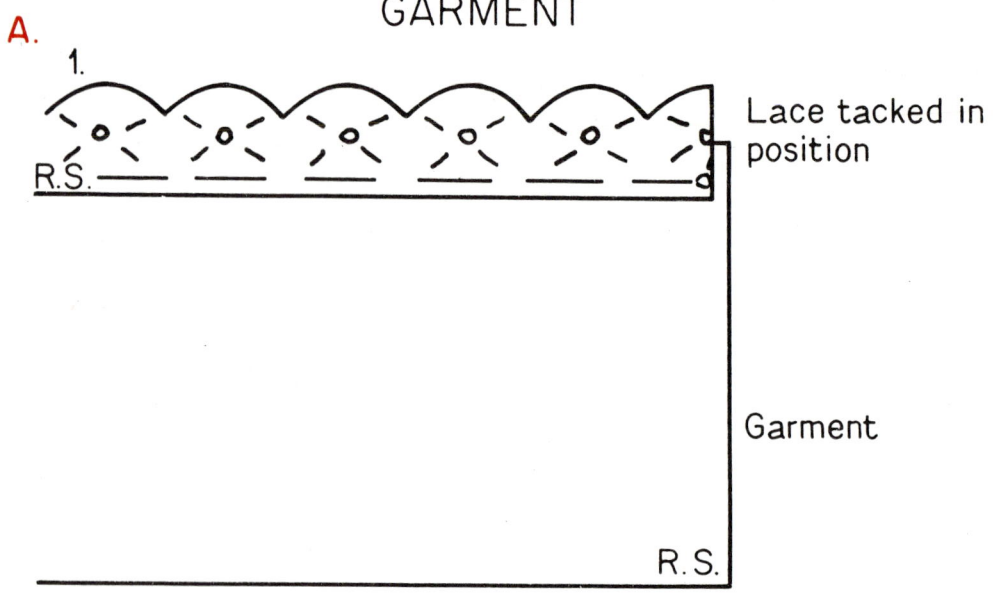

A.

1.

Lace tacked in position

R.S.

Garment

R.S.

2.
    Secure by one of the following method,–

        a) Hemming closely with silk or fine cotton.

        b) Chain stitch.

        c) Pin stitch.

        d) Satin stitch.

        e) Blanket stitch.

After application of lace, raw edges of garment may be trimmed and overcast.
If edges of garment are to be neatened before attaching lace, a very narrow hem should be turned and then machined, running-stitched or hemmed.

B. USING A CROSS-WAY STRIP.

1.

- Bias binding or cross-way strip
- Lace
- Garment

R.S.

- Lace
- Facing
- Garment

W.S.

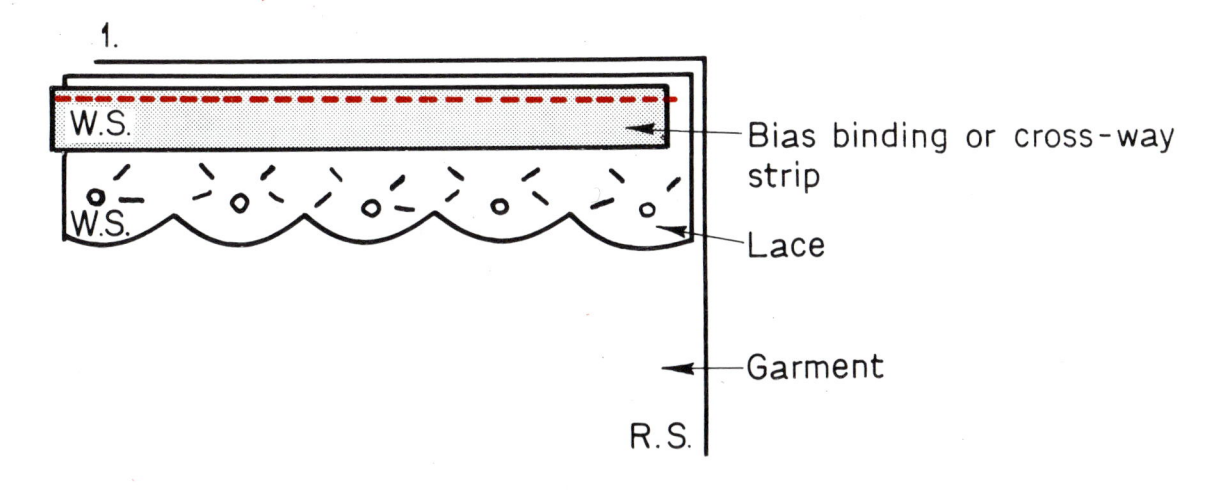

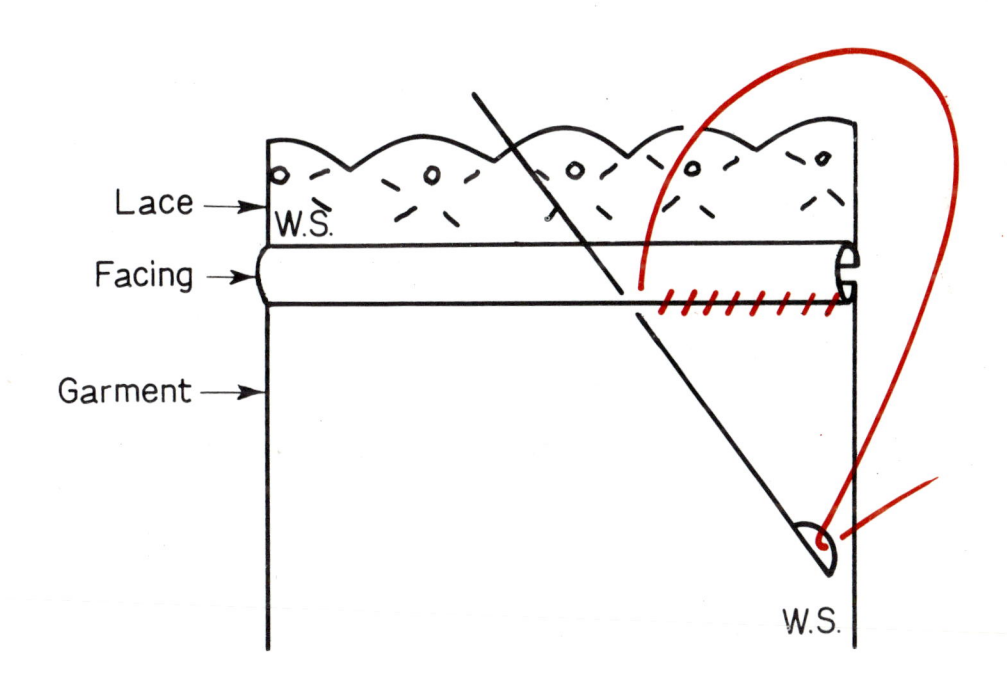

Lace may also be applied by means of, –

C. FAGGOTING.

D. WHIPPING ONTO A ROLLED HEM.

Openings

Use:
1 To allow garments to be put on easily and quickly
2 To allow garments to be made in a close-fitting style

Points to consider:
1 Style and position of openings in relation to style of garment which depends upon current fashion.
2 Type of fabric, finished effect required and whether it is an outer or under-garment.
3 Opening must be well and suitably placed and long enough. All this depends upon type of garment and closeness of fit
   Skirt placket – 7"–8" (18–20 cm)
   Dress side opening – $3\frac{1}{2}$" (9 cm) above and $4\frac{1}{2}$" (11 cm) below waist
   Dress back opening – 24" (60 cm)
   Full sleeve gathered into cuff – $2\frac{1}{2}$" (6·5 cm) in length and placed $2\frac{1}{2}$" (6·5 cm) to back of seam
   Long close-fitting sleeve – 3–4" (8–10 cm) in length
4 Opening may be worked
   a) in a slash, cut straight by the thread
   b) in a seam
5 Openings which overlap must overlap
   R. over L. for girls
   L. over R. for boys
6 Sufficient underwrap must be allowed to prevent gaping, and the opening must provide double fabric on which to sew the fastenings.
7 Both sides of opening must be equal and fixed at the end to keep it in position.
8 The opening must be flat, strong and neat, and it must keep its position when the garment is being worn.

Types of openings:
1 Where fabric is taken from the garment itself
   E.g. Equal hems, which are used chiefly on undergarments and on children's dresses with gathered skirts, where the pleat below the opening does not spoil style of garment
2 Where extra fabric is added to the garment
   One piece placket (continuous opening)
   Faced opening
   Wrap and facing opening
   Bound opening

CONTINUOUS OPENING
OR
ONE-PIECE PLACKET

1.

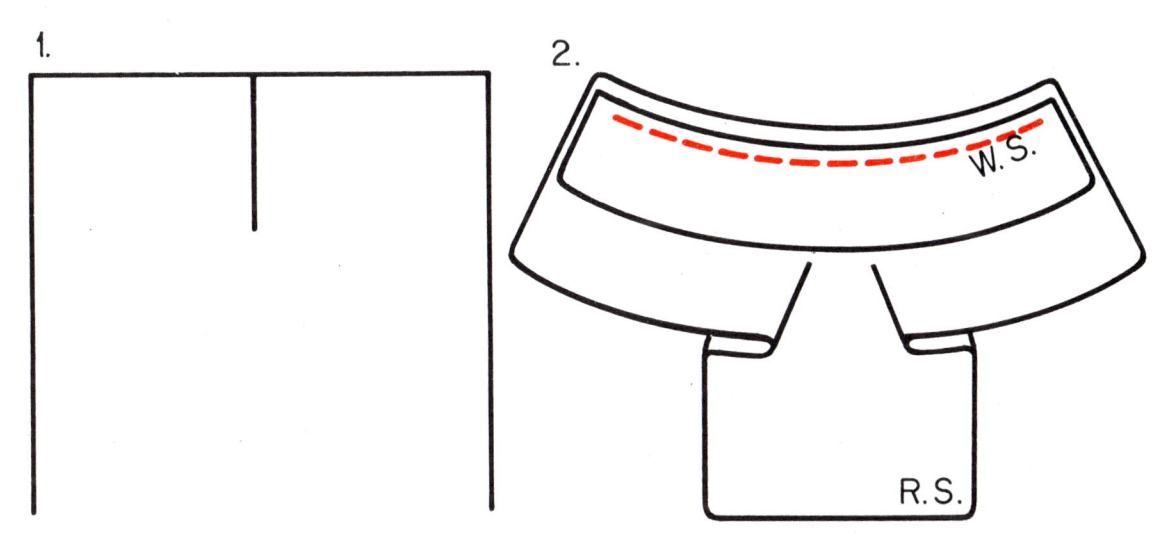

Cut slash straight by the thread. Cut strip of fabric also straight by the thread about 1½" (3·8cm) wide, length = 2x length of slash + 1" (2·5cm)

2.

Machine-stitch strip along edge of slash

3.

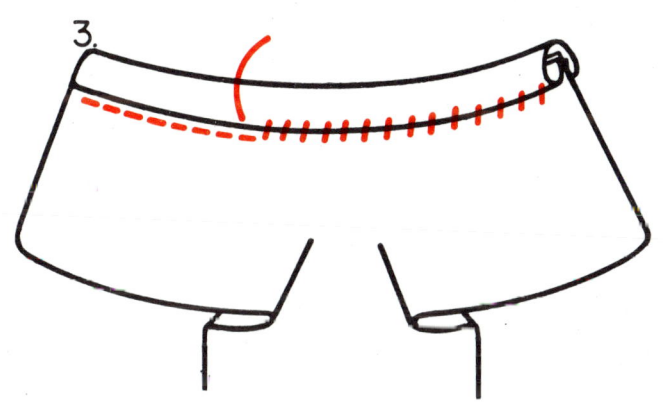

Turn a fold along strip on W.S. and hem in position by picking up stitches

4.

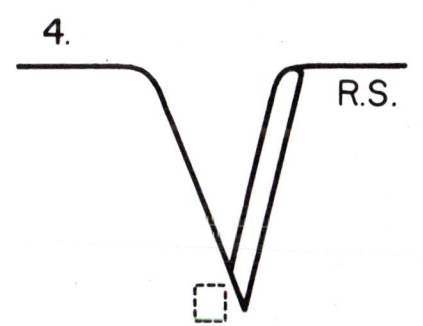

Opening pressed and stitched in position. Finished width = about ⅝" (1·5cm)

<u>Use</u>: *For all fine fabrics, on sleeves, necks, and sides of skirts and slacks.*

FACED OPENING
(In a slash)

1.

R.S.

W.S.

Turn in lower and side edges of facing and machine stitch along edge. Place facing on garment, right sides together. Stitch outline of opening in shape of a V. Slash between stitching.

2.

W.S

R.S.

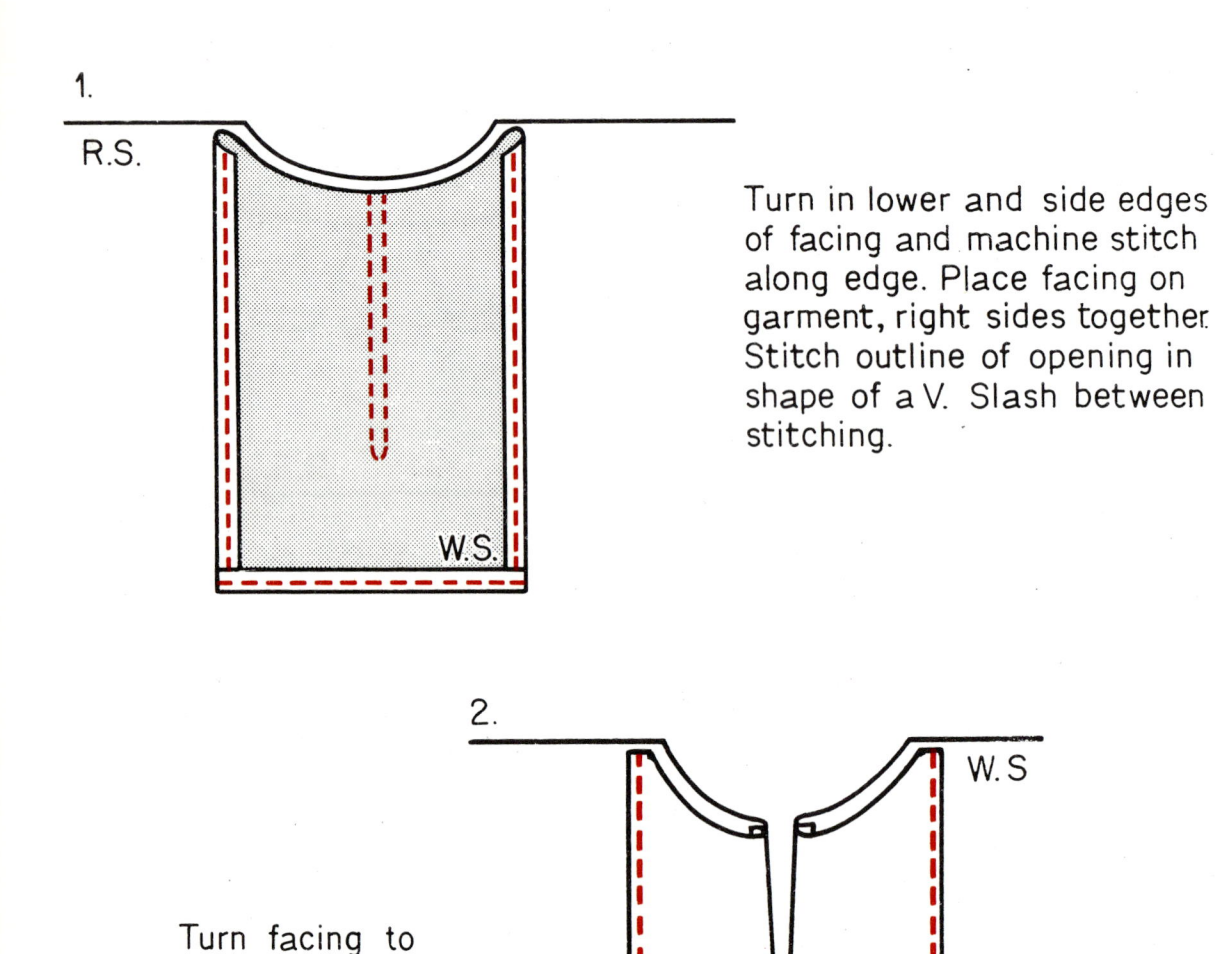

Turn facing to inside and press

<u>Use.</u> For neck openings and on long sleeves gathered into a cuff

BOUND OPENING
(In a slash)

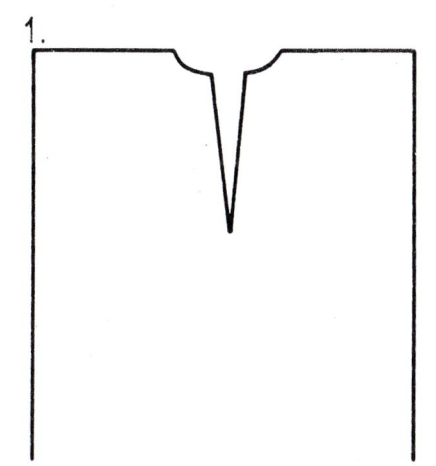

1.

Cut slash straight by the thread. Cut binding on the true bias, width = 1", (2·5 cm) length = 2 × length of slash + 1", (2·5 cm)

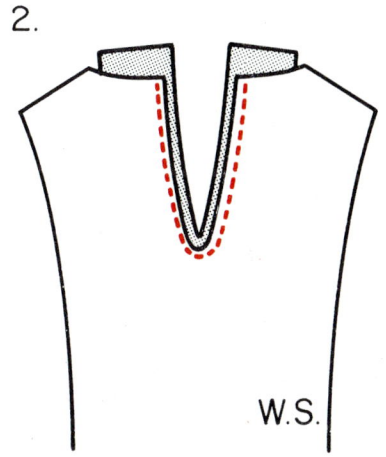

2.

W.S.

Machine-stitch binding along edge of slash with right sides together.

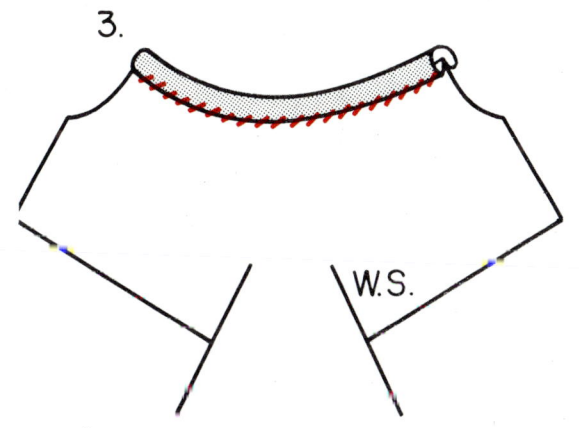

3.

W.S.

Hem binding in position on W.S. by picking up machine-stitching.

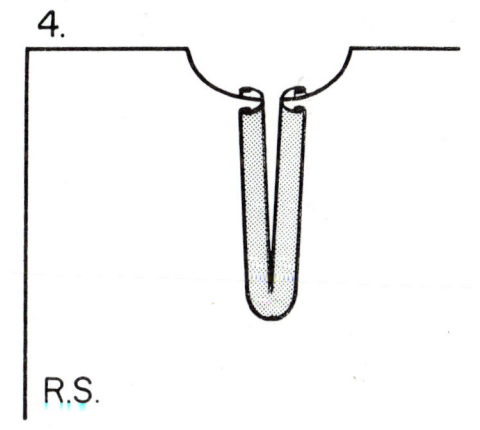

4.

R.S.

Bound opening pressed in position on R.S.

<u>Use</u>: *For neck and sleeve openings*

WRAP AND FACING OPENING
(In a seam)

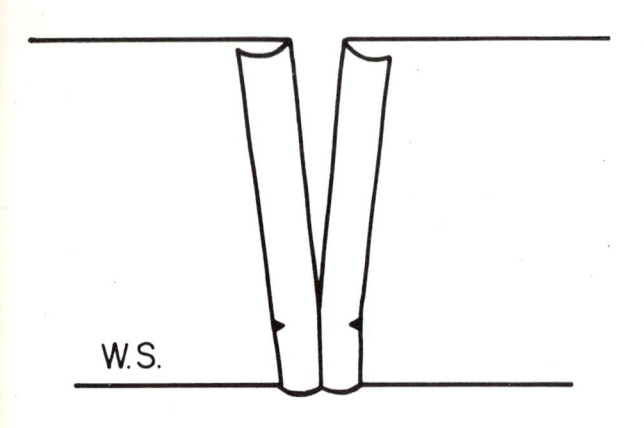

W.S.

Seam and opening on W.S.

Stitch facing along seam line of garment, and slip-hem in position on W.S.

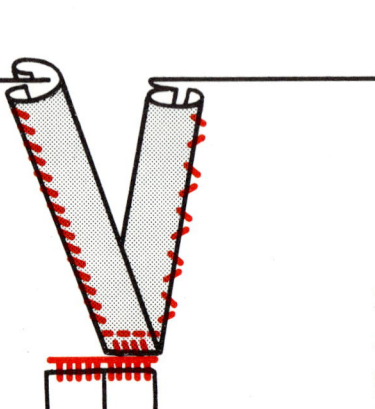

W.S.

W.S.

Stitch binding along seam line and hem in position on W.S. by picking up machine-stitches. Neaten all raw edges with blanket stitches

Use: For side-openings of dresses shirts, pyjamas and slacks.

Fastenings

Points to remember:
1 Choice of fastening depends upon:
   a) Type of garment
   b) Fabric – weight, texture and whether washable or not
   c) Whether the fastening is to be invisible, or visible and decorative – thus forming part of the style of the garment
2 Fastenings must be so placed that the garment keeps its position when worn, and the opening does not gape.
3 Fastenings should always be stitched on to double fabric for strength and durability.

Types of fastenings:
1 Buttons and buttonholes (worked or bound) – for openings which overlap.
2 Buttons and loops (worked or rouleau) – for openings which meet edge to edge.
3 Hooks and Eyes or Worked Bars – for openings which meet or overlap.
4 Press studs (or snap fasteners) – for openings which overlap only.
5 Zip fasteners – for openings which meet edge to edge.
6 Tapes (or Ribbon to tie) and Faced Slots – for edges which meet.
7 Eyelet holes and cords – for openings which meet edge to edge.
8 Toggles and braid – for openings which meet or overlap.
9 Velcro (which consists of two surfaces – one of a series of hooks and one of loops, and which, when pressed together, remain stuck until peeled open again) – suitable only for openings which overlap.

Buttons

1. Mark position of button – when fastened, the button will be at the outer end of the buttonhole. Thread should match button rather than garment.
2. Begin with backstitches on right side of garment, then sew through button and back into fabric. These stitches should be fairly loose, so that a stem or shank is formed between button and garment. After sewing the button, the thread should be wound around the threads under the button to form a firm stem.
3. Finish off neatly by means of a bar on W.S.

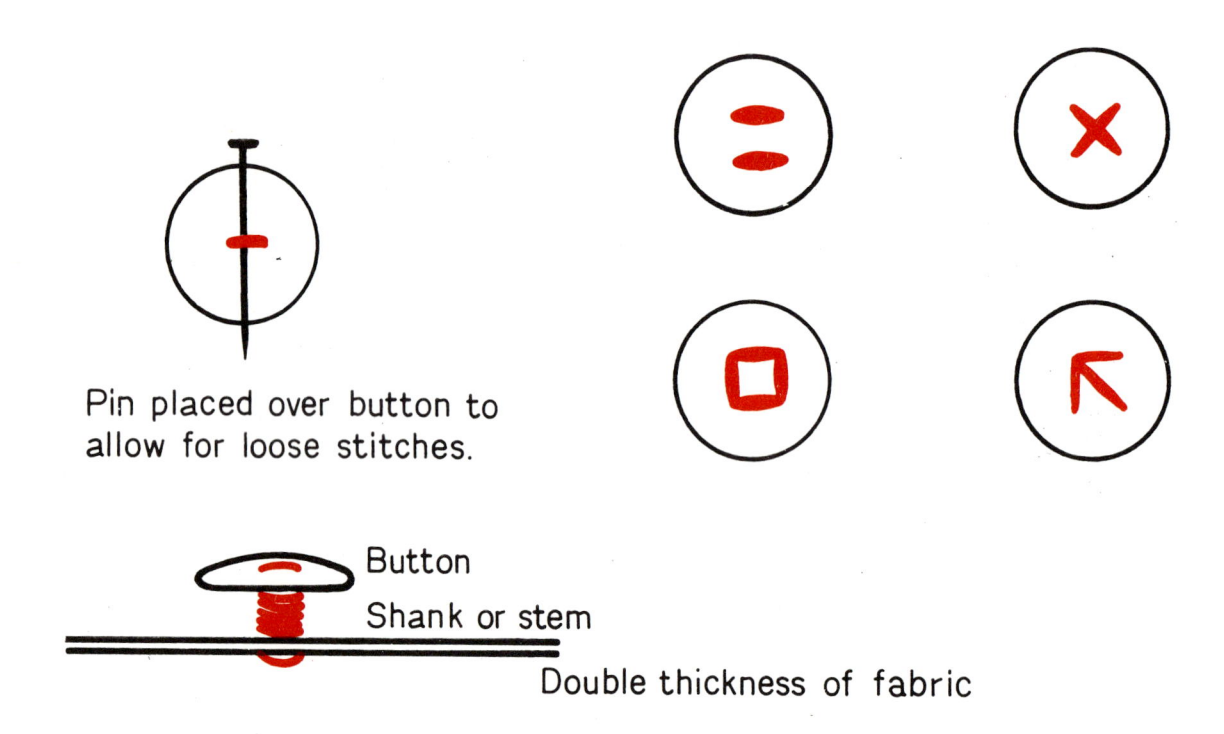

Pin placed over button to allow for loose stitches.

Button
Shank or stem
Double thickness of fabric

WORKED BUTTONHOLE

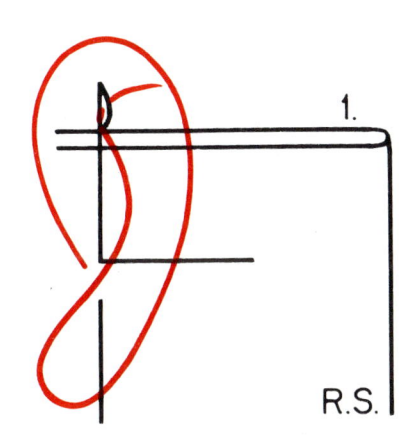

Position = not less than $\frac{1}{2}$ width of button from the edge. Cut buttonhole straight by the thread. Width = width of button + $\frac{1"}{8}$ (·25 cm)

Bring needle out at left hand corner and buttonhole stitch L to R as far as right hand corner.

Oversew 5-7 stitches around corner, then buttonhole-stitch to end

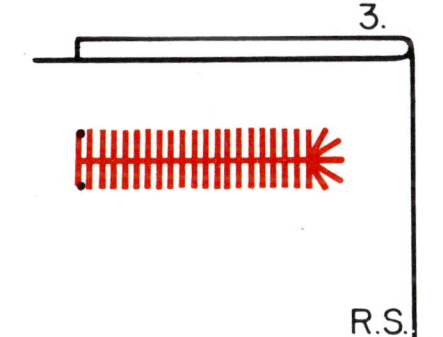

Work 3 straight stitches at last corner and work buttonhole stitch along these on R.S. and W.S.

Finished buttonhole

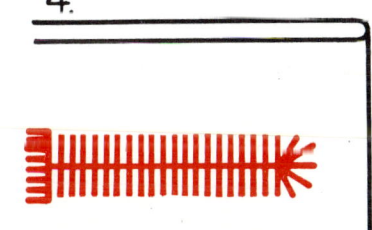

BOUND BUTTONHOLE

1.

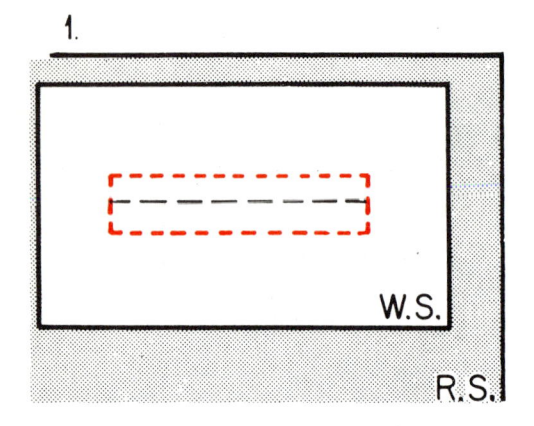

W.S.
R.S.

Mark position of buttonhole with tacking. Machine stitch $\frac{1}{8}"$ (·25cm) above and below tacking, connecting stitching at ends.

2.

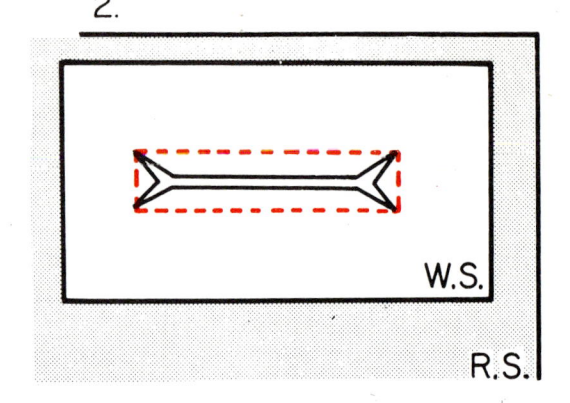

W.S.
R.S.

Slash between stitches to within $\frac{1}{8}"$ (·25cm) from ends, clipping ends diagonally. Push strip through to W.S. of garment.

3.

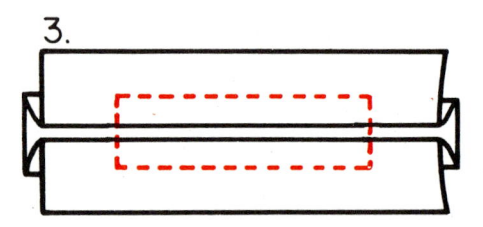

Form a pleat on W.S. Tack. Stab stitch or machine around buttonhole from R.S.

4.

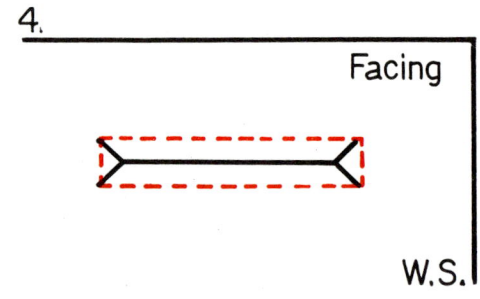

Facing
W.S.

Mark buttonhole on facing and slash as before. Fold turnings back to W.S.

5.

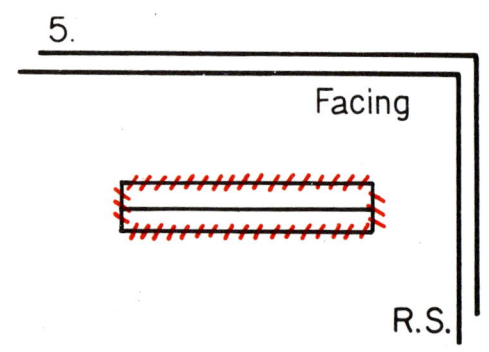

Facing
R.S.

Slip-stitch or hem facing to buttonhole on inside.

6.

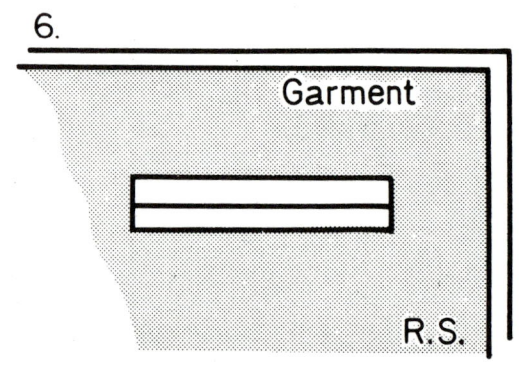

Garment
R.S.

Finished buttonhole

WORKED LOOPS.

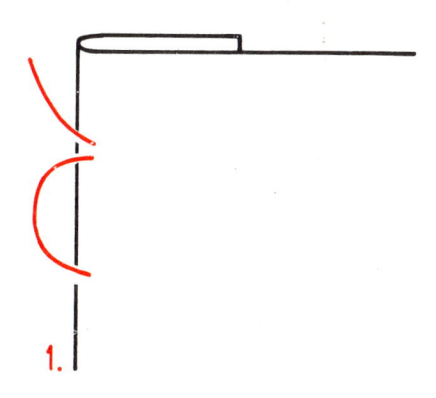

1. Work three loose stitches on edge of fold which should be along fitting line.

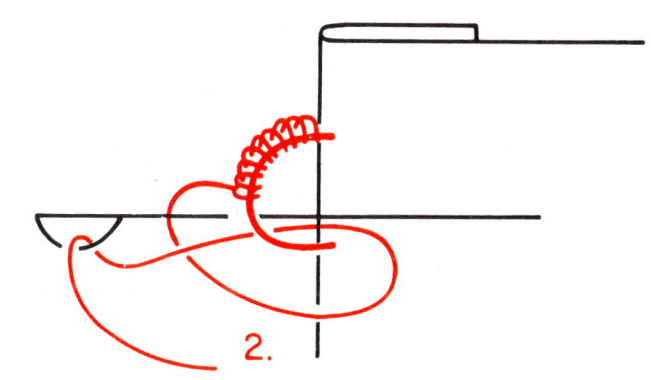

2. With eye of needle towards worker, blanket stitch firmly to form a loop. Finish off securely.

ROULEAU LOOPS

1. Prepare a long narrow strip cut on the cross.

2. Place rouleau strip on R.S. of garment so that loops protrude beyond fitting line. Tack firmly. Place facing in position and machine-stitch along fitting line securing the loops at the same time.

3. Turn facing over so that loops protrude from the edge.

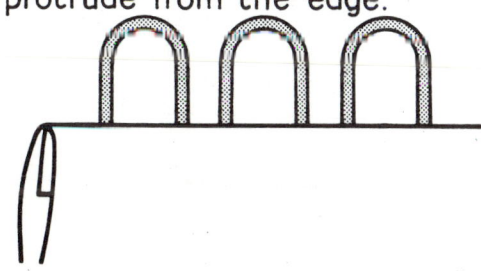

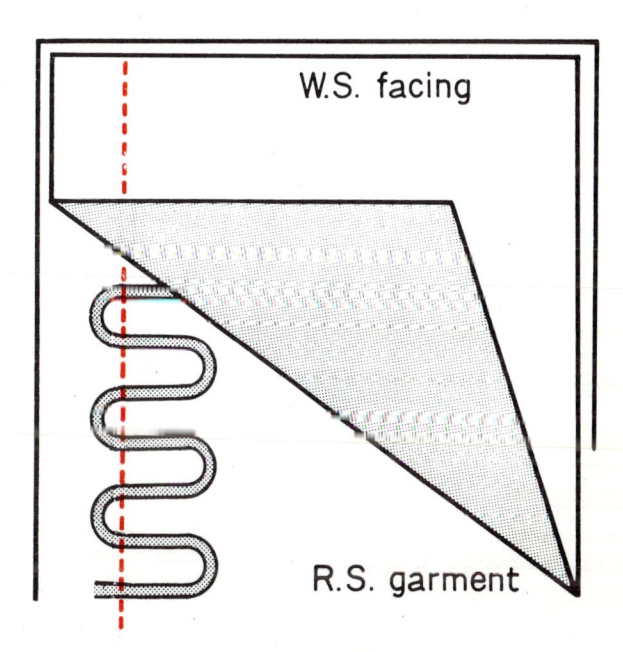

W.S. facing

R.S. garment

ZIP FASTENERS

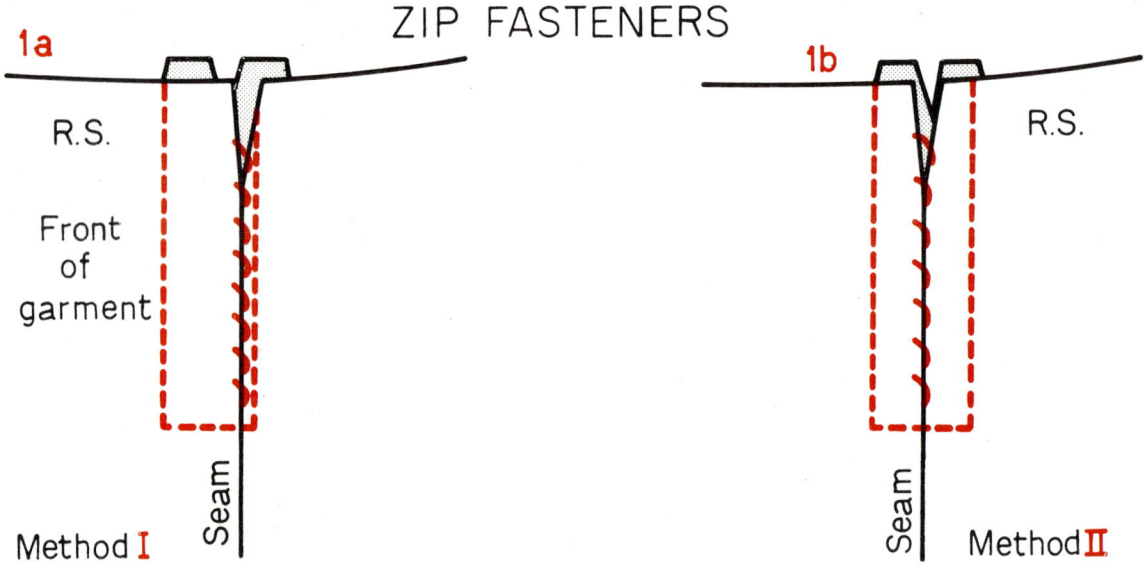

Method I

1. Tack seam allowance to W.S. along length of opening so that fitting lines are edge to edge.
2. Tack zip in position – back of garment close to zip. Front of garment overlapping metal part of zip completely and with metal top of zip $\frac{1}{2}$" (1·25 cm) below seam line of garment.
3. Baste folded edges together so that they do not gape.
4. Machine and finish off securely.

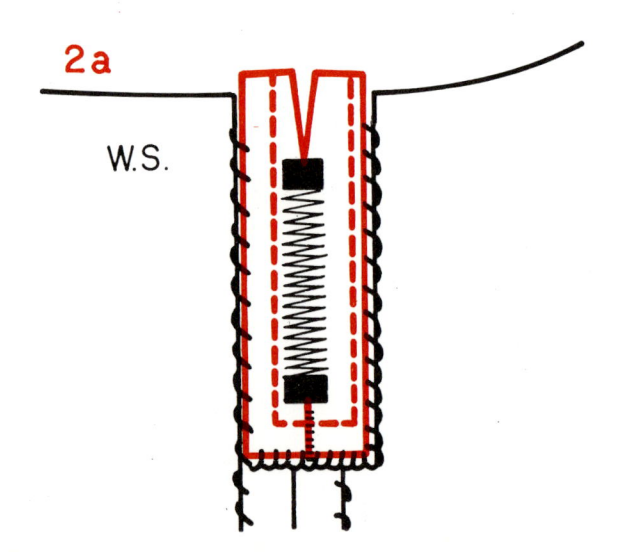

Method II

1. Tack seam allowance to W.S. along length of opening so that fitting lines are edge to edge.
2. Tack zip in position – metal top of zip $\frac{1}{2}$" (1·25 cm) below seam line of garment and with back and front fitting line meeting exactly on centre line of zip.
3. Baste folded edges together to avoid gaping.
4. Machine stitch and finish off securely.

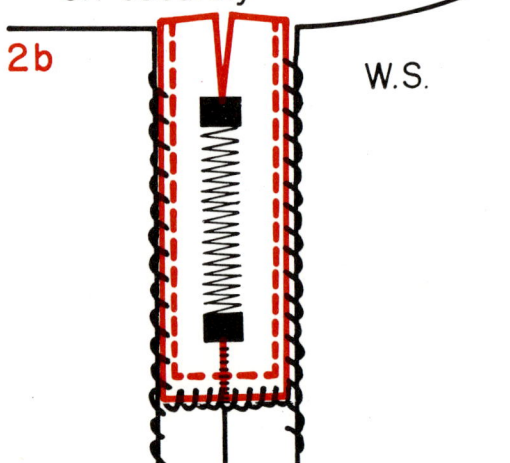

HOOK AND EYE

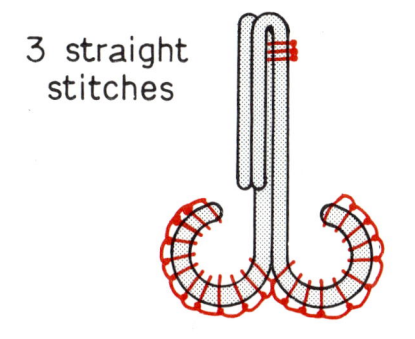

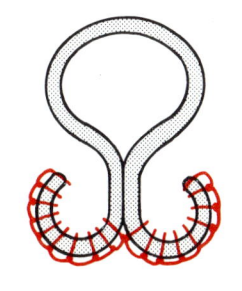

3 straight stitches

Hook and eye stitched in position by means of buttonhole-stitch or oversewing.

Worked bar.

1. Work 5 or 6 straight threads on R.S. and W.S.

   Blanket stitch threads firmly to form a bar on both R.S. and W.S.

R.S. and W.S.

PRESS STUDS OR SNAP FASTENERS

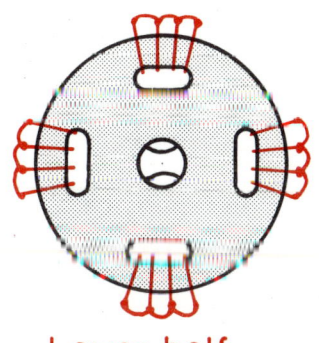

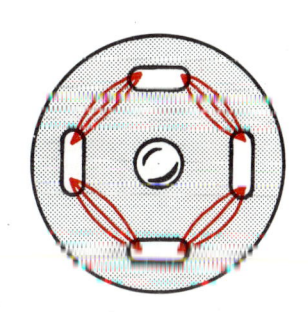

Lower half

Top half

Buttonhole stitch or oversew in position.

TAPES

1.

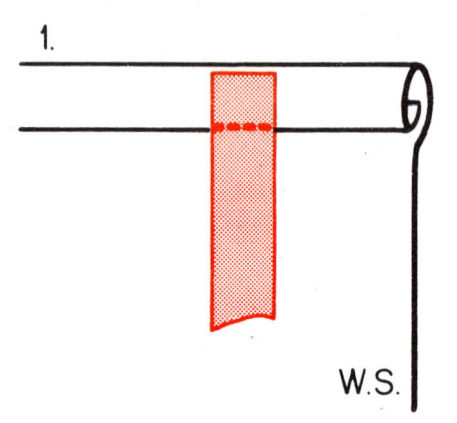

W.S.

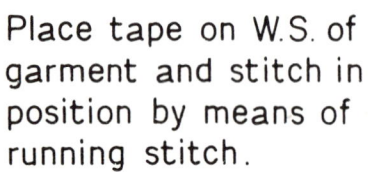

Place tape on W.S. of garment and stitch in position by means of running stitch.

2.

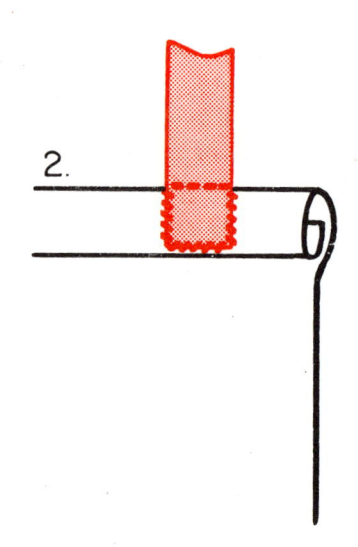

Fold tape over. Hem 3 sides on W.S. and oversew top edge on R.S.

This method is also used for sewing on shoulder straps.

If the tape is placed on R.S., then machine-stitching is used along 4 sides.

3.

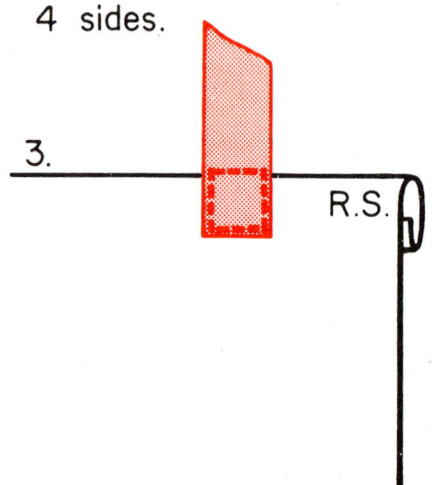

R.S.

Tape loop at a corner

W.S.

Machine-stitch along 4 sides on R.S.

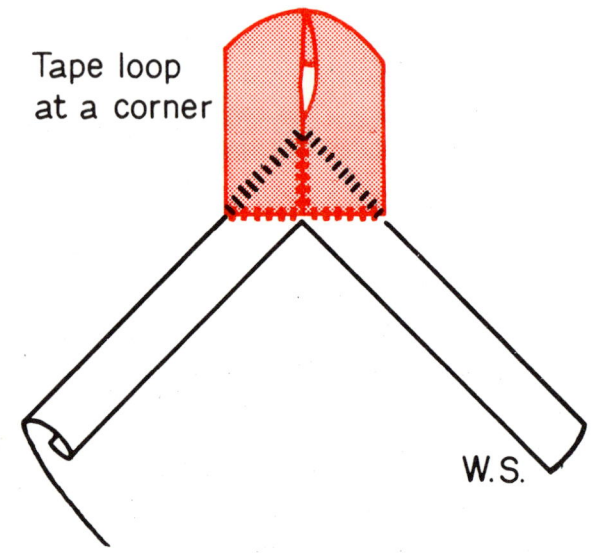

Hemming on W.S. oversewing 2 sides on R.S.

EYELET HOLES

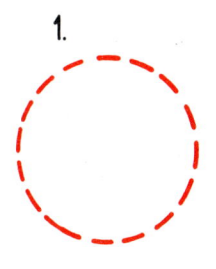

1. Outline with running stitch.

2. Pierce a hole with a stiletto or hole is cut open from centre.

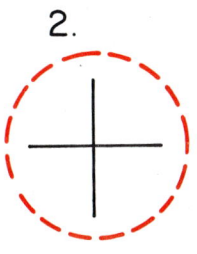

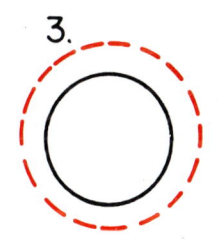

3. Raw edges are turned to W.S.

4. Edge finished with loop stitch or overcasting

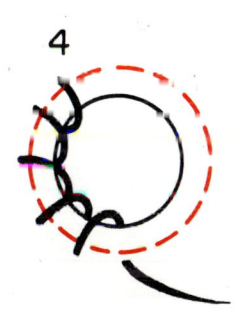

FACED SLOT

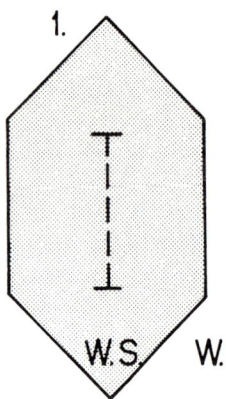

1. Mark position of slot. Place facing on W.S. of garment with threads matching. Tack.

W.S. of garment

2. Machine stitch around tacking. Cut open between stitches.

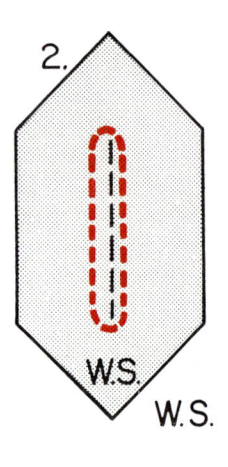

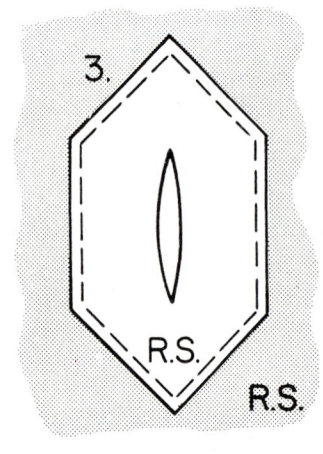

3. Push through to R.S. turn in raw edges

4. Machine stitch in position on R.S.

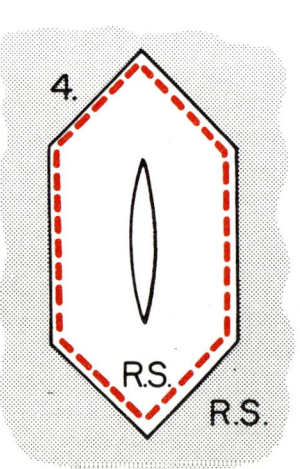

A BELT
(Unstiffened)

1.

Machine stitch along seam line leaving a gap of about 3" (7.5cm) in the centre.

2.

Press seam open flat, and machine stitch a straight or pointed end as desired. Trim away any surplus material, especially around point.

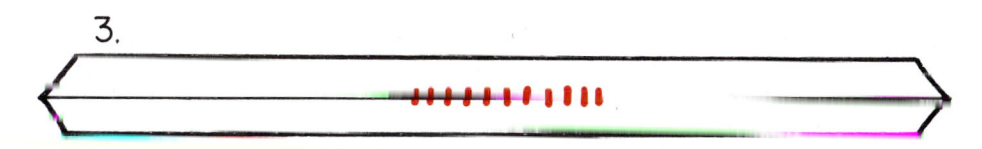

3.

Push ends through gap to R.S. Close gap by means of oversewing. Press carefully.

A BELT LOOP

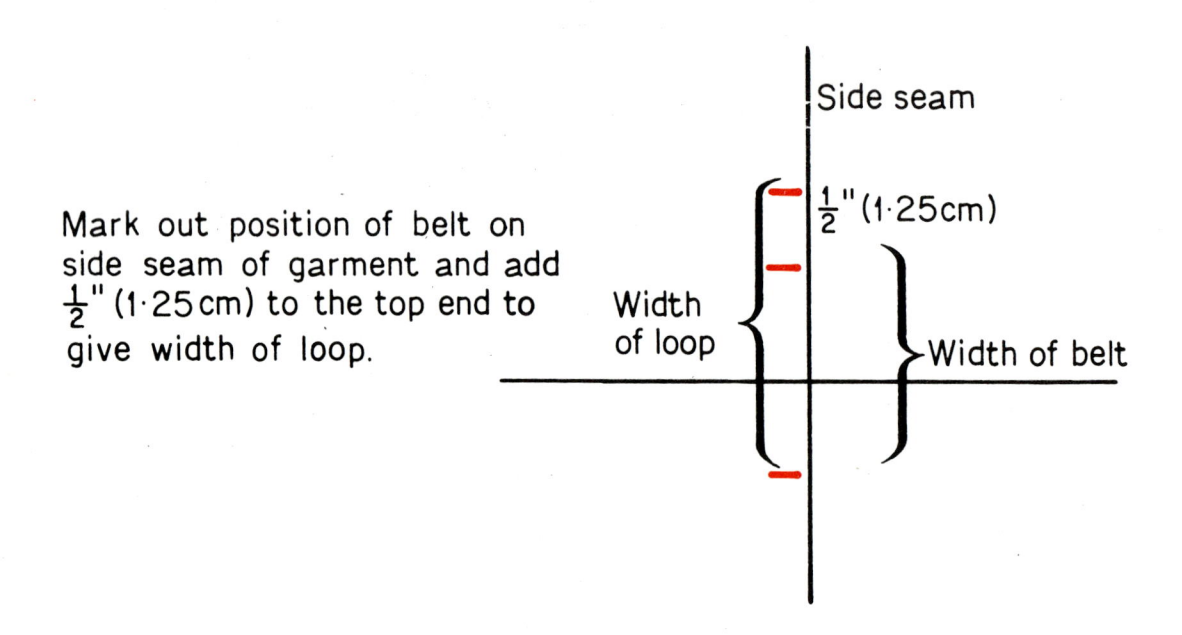

Mark out position of belt on side seam of garment and add $\frac{1}{2}$" (1.25 cm) to the top end to give width of loop.

Width of loop

Side seam

$\frac{1}{2}$" (1.25 cm)

Width of belt

Work 5 or 6 straight stitches on R.S., using buttonhole twist or embroidery thread, such as coton à broder

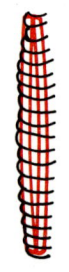

Blanket stitch threads firmly to form a bar. Finish off neatly on W.S.

An alternative method is to use a rouleau strip which must be neatened at both ends before being attached to the garment.

Fullness

Use:
 1 For ease of movement, at the same time keeping a good outline
 2 For decorative effect

Type of fullness used depends upon:
 1 Fabric – weight, texture, whether washable or not
 2 Type of garment – evening wear, afternoon, country or townwear
 3 The wearer

Fullness may be introduced by:
 1 *Use of bias*
    flare, gores, godets
 2 *Folding of fabric*
    pleats, tucks, darts
 3 *Drawing up of fabric*
    gathering, smocking, ruching, shirring

A. FOLDING OF MATERIAL

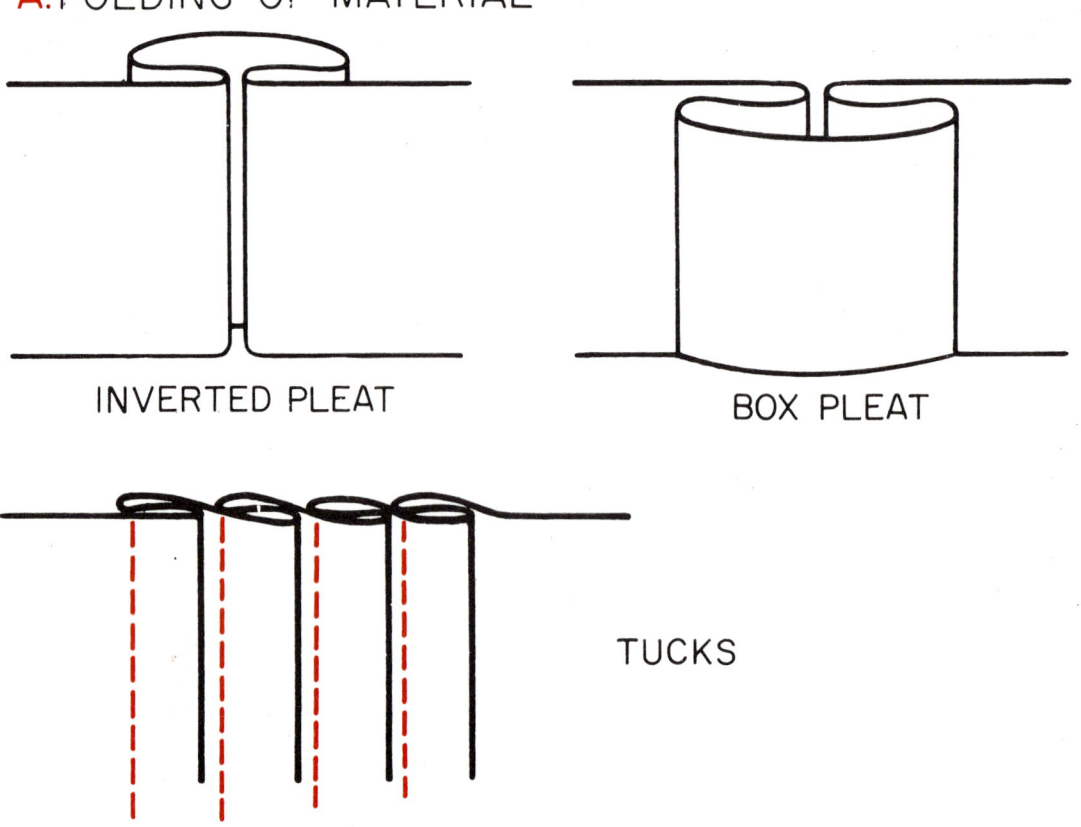

INVERTED PLEAT

BOX PLEAT

TUCKS

Darts are used extensively on outer and undergarments as a practical method of disposing of fullness rather than as a decoration. Work by stitching from the wide end, moving gradually towards the point. The last two or three stitches lying parrallel and as near as possible to the edge. Machine over the edge and finish off securely. Press carefully

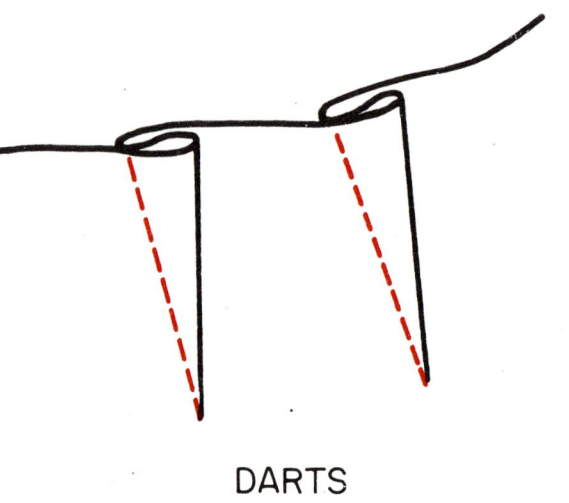

DARTS

B. USE OF BIAS

Flare

Gores

C. DRAWING UP MATERIAL

GATHERING

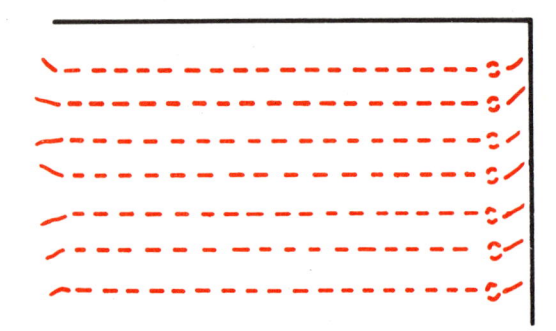

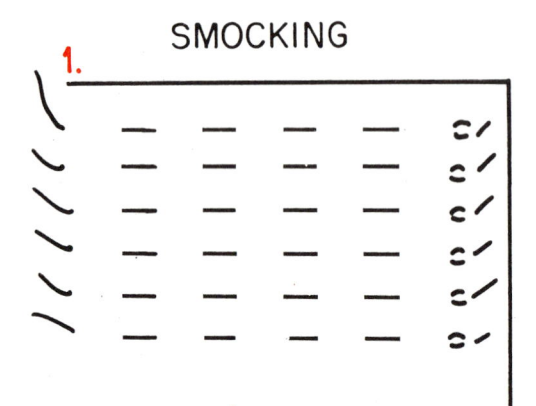

GAUGING

SMOCKING

1. Material is drawn up in regular lines on W.S.

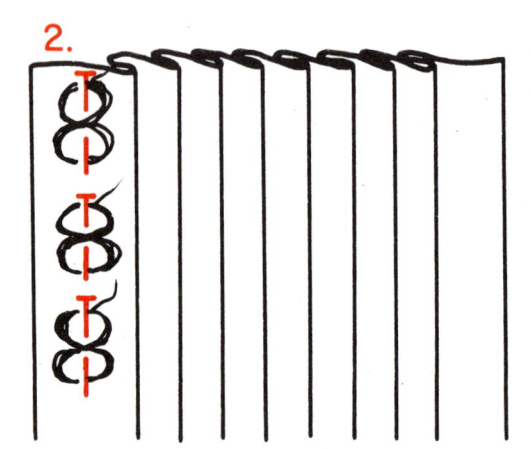

2. Threads are drawn up and folds are stroked to form even and regular pleats on W.S. and R.S.

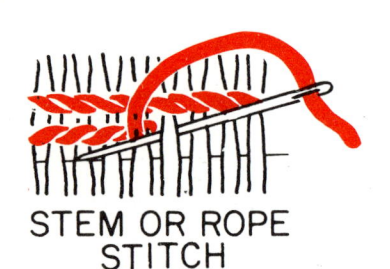

STEM OR ROPE STITCH

CABLE OR BASKET STITCH

SURFACE HONEYCOMBE STITCH

3. Work embroidery stitches along pleats on R.S. to form a pattern.

YOKES

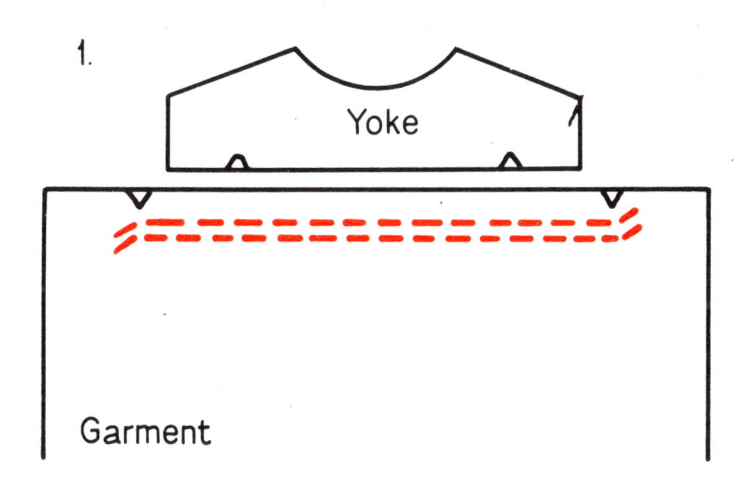

1. Gather along seam line between notches on garment.

2. Draw up threads till garment fits yoke. Tack and machine-stitch both along seam line, keeping the gathers uppermost while machining.

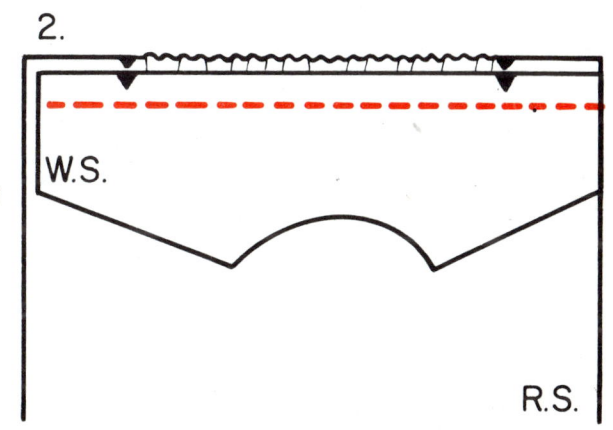

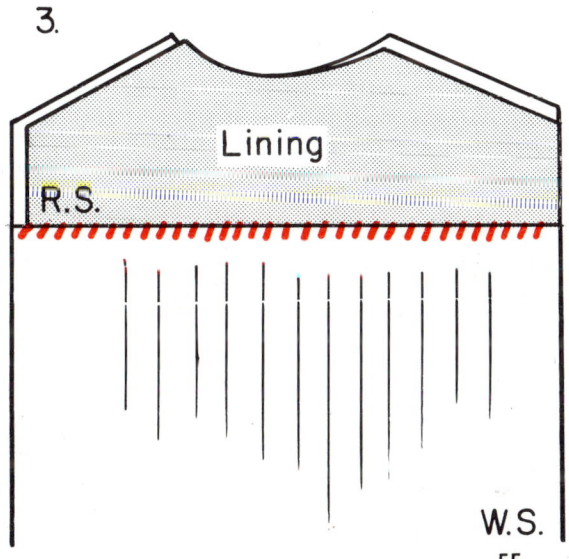

3. Turn a fold along seam line of lining and hem in position by picking up machine stitches worked in No. 2.

SETTING A CUFF ON A SLEEVE

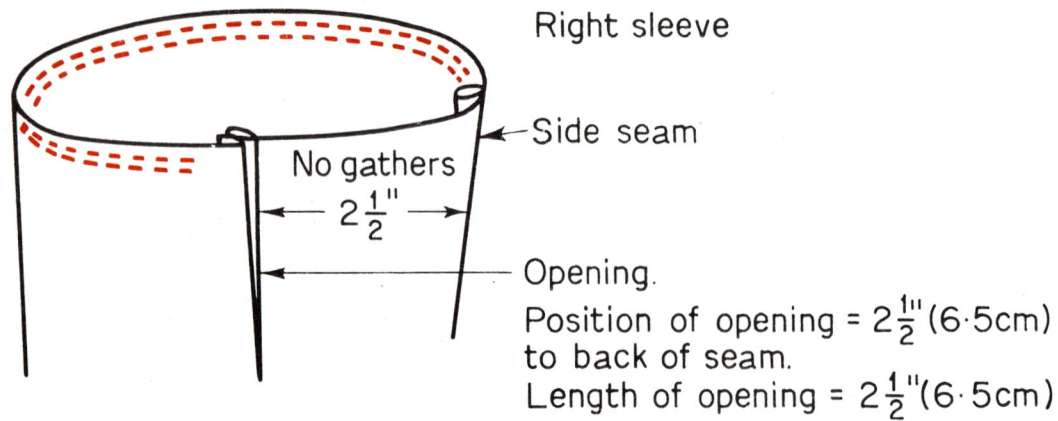

Right sleeve

Side seam

No gathers 2½"

Opening.
Position of opening = 2½" (6·5cm) to back of seam.
Length of opening = 2½" (6·5cm)

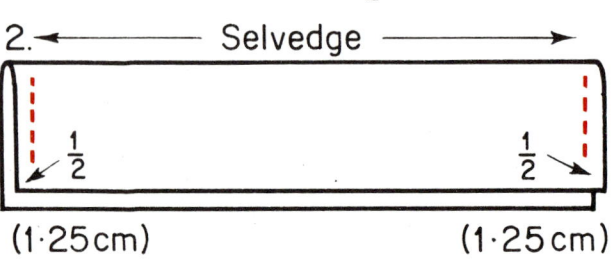

2. ← Selvedge →

½ ½
(1·25cm) (1·25cm)

Prepare cuff by folding in half lengthwise. Stitch along seam line on both ends to within ½" (1·25 cm) of edge. Turn to R.S.

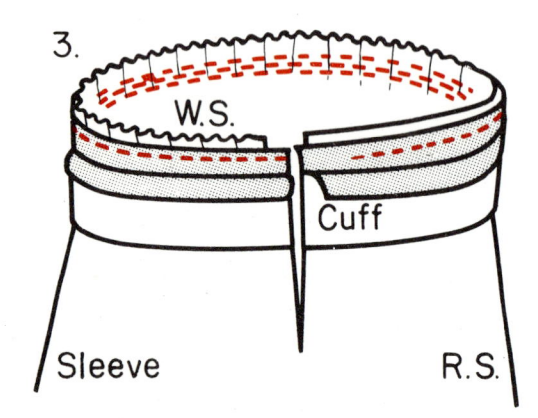

3.

W.S.

Cuff

Sleeve   R.S.

Tack one edge of cuff to sleeve, easing the gathers evenly to fit cuff. Machine-stitch along seam line. Trim away surplus material.

Turn to W.S. of sleeve. Turn a fold along seam line of cuff and hem in position by picking up machine-stitching.

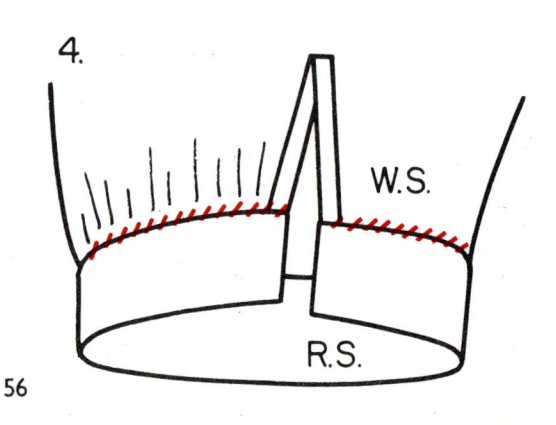

4.

W.S.

R.S.

SETTING ON A COLLAR

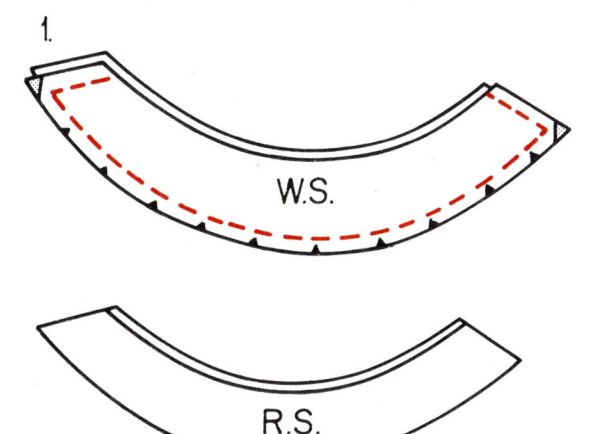

1. Tack interfacing to underside of collar. Prepare collar by tacking and machining along fitting line, leaving inner curve unstitched. Snip edge at intervals. Trim away surplus material. Turn to R.S. and press

Prepare facings by joining back facing to front facings at shoulders. Finish off, neaten and press. Turn a fold to W.S. along outer edge of facings. Machine along the edge and press.

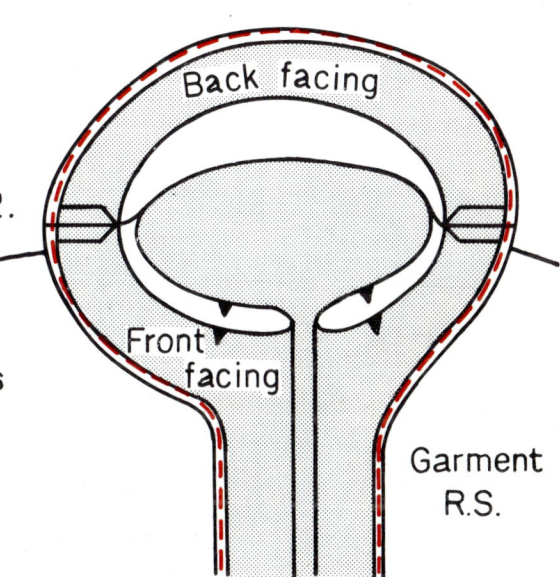

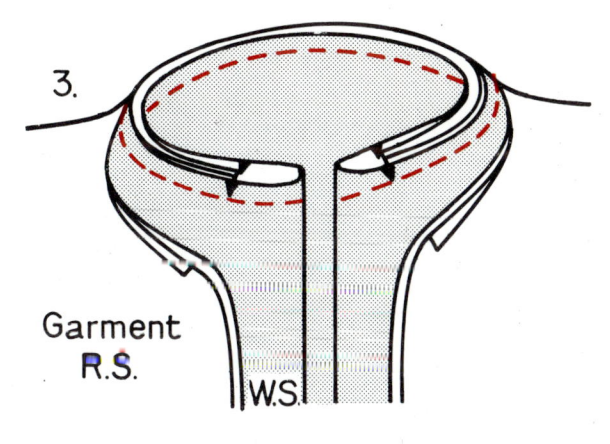

2. Sandwich collar in between facings and garment, matching C.F. and C.B. Tack and machine firmly. Trim away surplus material. Snip at intervals to allow for curve.

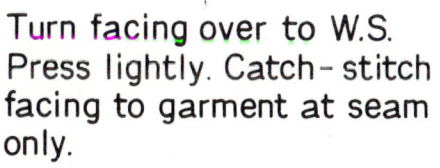

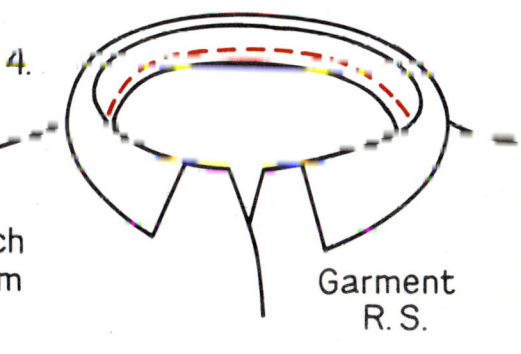

3. Turn facing over to W.S. Press lightly. Catch-stitch facing to garment at seam only.

Setting in a sleeve

Preparation of Garment:
1 All seams leading to armhole should be finished, pressed and neatened.
2 Armhole line and notches should be clearly marked and corrected if necessary.

Preparation of Sleeve:

Sleeves should be worked as a pair

1 All fitting lines, balance marks and straight of thread clearly marked.
2 Seams should be securely stitched, neatened and pressed.
3 Two rows of gathering worked along top of sleeve, extending from notch to notch—one row on fitting-line and one row $\frac{1}{8}''$ (·25 cm) away between fitting-line and edge.
The sleeve should always be bigger than the armhole and therefore it is always necessary to ease the sleeve into the armhole.

Setting:
1 Pin at underarm seam and balance marks.
2 Pin horizontally between notches, where there is no gathering.
3 Draw up gathering threads evenly and ease to fit armhole. Pin vertically with the folds along the fitting line.
There should be slightly more fullness to the back.
4 Tack firmly in position.
5 Tack and machine securely along fitting line with gathers facing worker. Finish off firmly.
6 Trim raw edges to $\frac{3}{8}''$ (1 cm) and overcast or bind with soft bias binding.
7 Remove gathering threads and press.

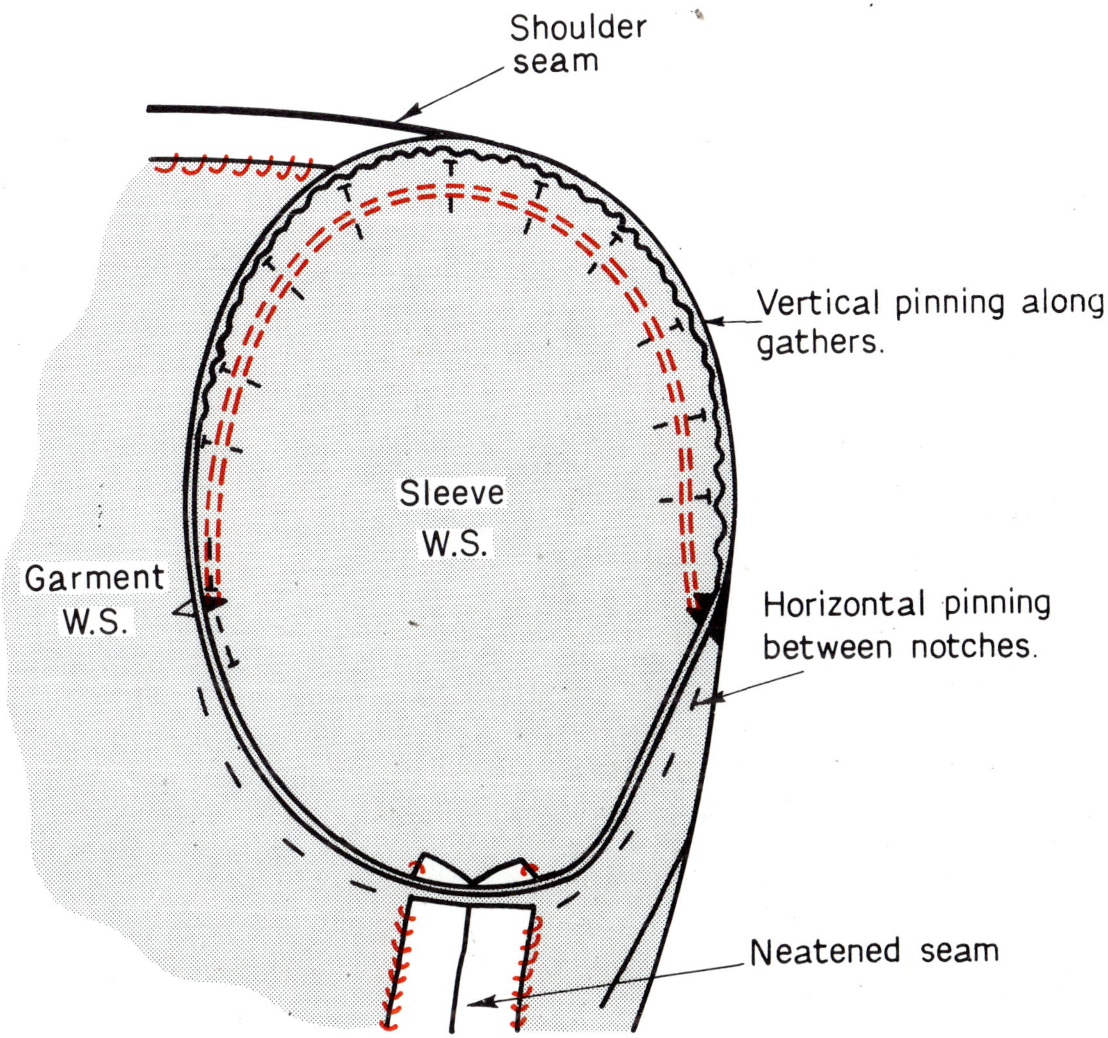
Shoulder
seam
Vertical pinning along
gathers.
Sleeve
W.S.
Garment
W.S.
Horizontal pinning
between notches.
Neatened seam

SETTING A WAISTBAND ON A SKIRT.

1. Snip

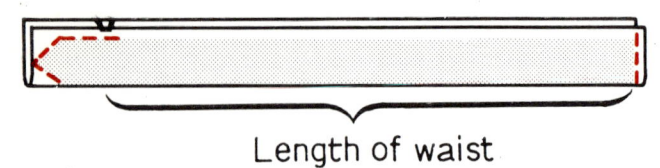

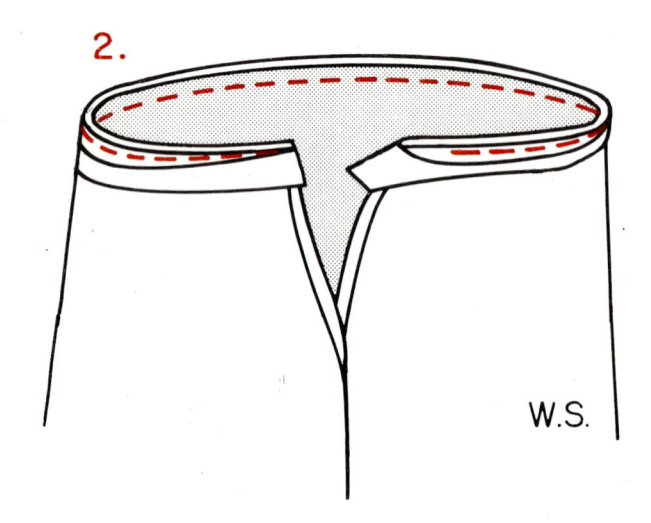

Length of waist

Cut waistband: width = 2x finished width + 1" (2·5cm) length = measurement of waist + 3" (8cm). Cut interfacing or stiffening same measurements as finished band. Tack onto W.S. band. Machine-stitch overlapping end to form point and one straight end to within $\frac{1"}{2}$ (1·25 cm) of raw edges. Trim away surplus fabric. Turn to R.S. Press.

2.

W.S.

Tack and machine band onto fitting line of skirt so that pointed end protrudes and overlaps R. over L. Trim away surplus fabric. Turn band over to outside.

Turn a fold along seam line of band. Tack and machine in position so that it covers line of stitching showing through from W.S. Finish off neatly. Work buttonhole on pointed end and sew button to match on straight end.

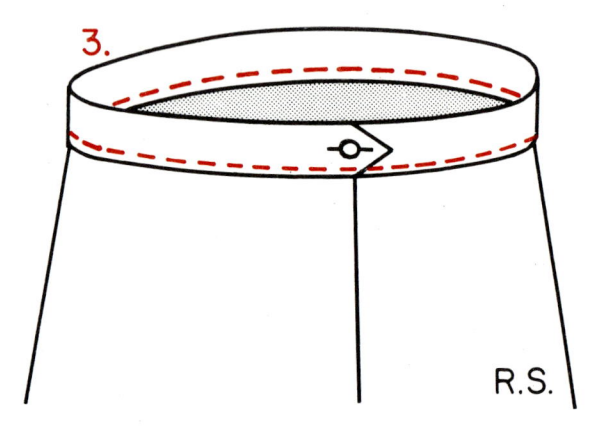

3.

R.S.

Band may be machined on outside first and then turned over to inside and hemmed in position.

POCKETS

STYLE OF POCKETS.

Patch pocket — used on dresses, overalls etc.

Piped pocket (Looks similar to a large bound buttonhole on R.S.) used on tailored garments.

Welt pocket — such as ones used on waistcoats.

Flap pocket — used on overcoats etc.

Slit pocket — used on capes.

Dart or seam pocket — used on slacks, skirts etc.

A SIMPLE PATCH POCKET.

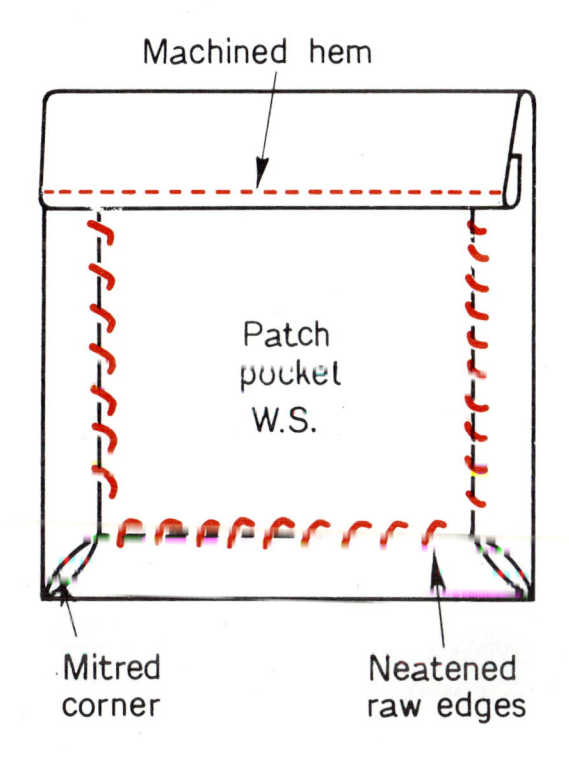

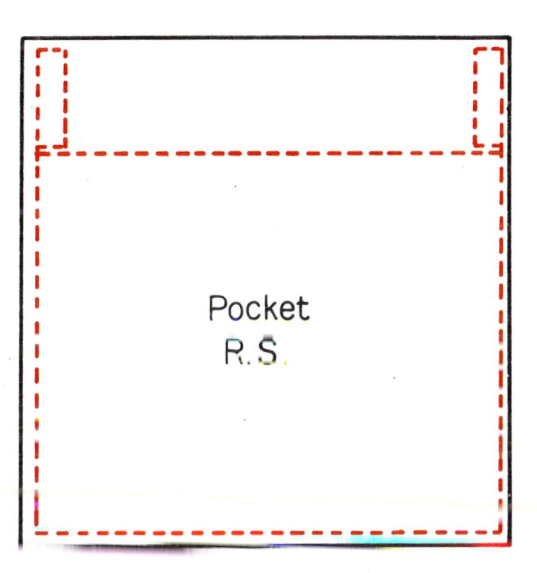

Machined hem

Patch pocket W.S.

Mitred corner

Neatened raw edges

Pocket R.S.

Patch pocket machined in position on R.S. of garment.

ARROW-HEAD

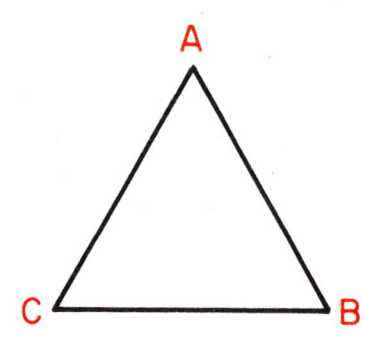

```
       A
      / \
     /   \
    /     \
   /       \
  C---------B
```

1. Mark arrow-head clearly with tacking cotton

2. Using buttonhole twist or any other soft thread, all stitching is worked from R. to L.

3. Start at A making a very small stitch.

4. Put in at B, out at C.

5. Put needle in just below last stitch at A and carry on in same way, putting needle in just below last stitch all the time.

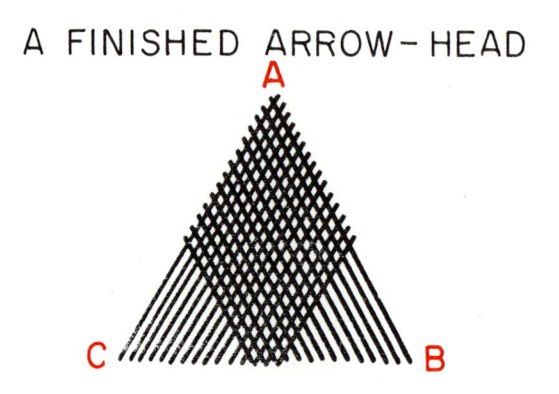

A FINISHED ARROW-HEAD

Darning

General Rules:
1 The thread used must correspond with the fabric, e.g. cotton on cotton, with special regard to colour, texture and thickness.
2 Darning is generally worked on W.S. A long fine darning needle is most suitable for the work.
3 All cuts should first of all be drawn together with fish-bone stitch.
4 Working parallel with the threads, loops must be left at the end of each row to allow for shrinkage.
5 Keep outline of darn a definite shape, but it should not be in line with either the selvedge or weft threads as this would bring undue strain on one thread.
6 The darn should be large enough to cover hole and all worn parts. Attempt to imitate as closely as possible the texture of the material being darned.
7 Darn along the selvedge threads first.
8 Double darning should be worked over the hole and thin places surrounding the hole.

THIN PLACE OR PREVENTATIVE DARNS

These are worked when an article has worn thin but before a hole has appeared.

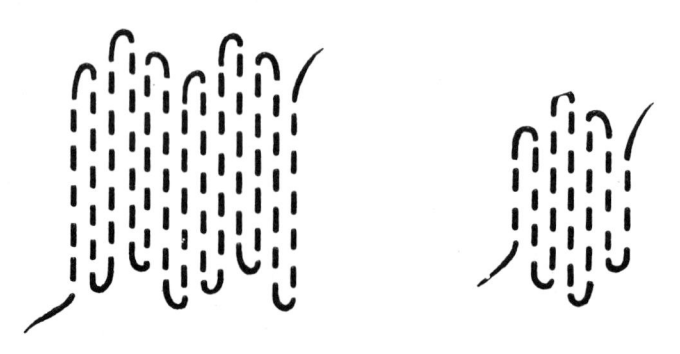

DARNING A HOLE

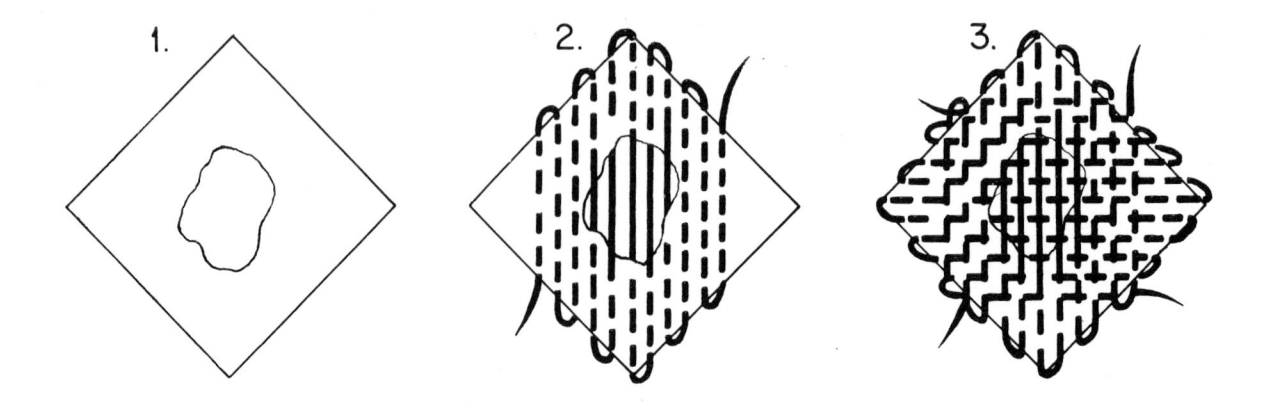

1.

2.

3.

DARNING A HOLE IN KNITTED FABRIC

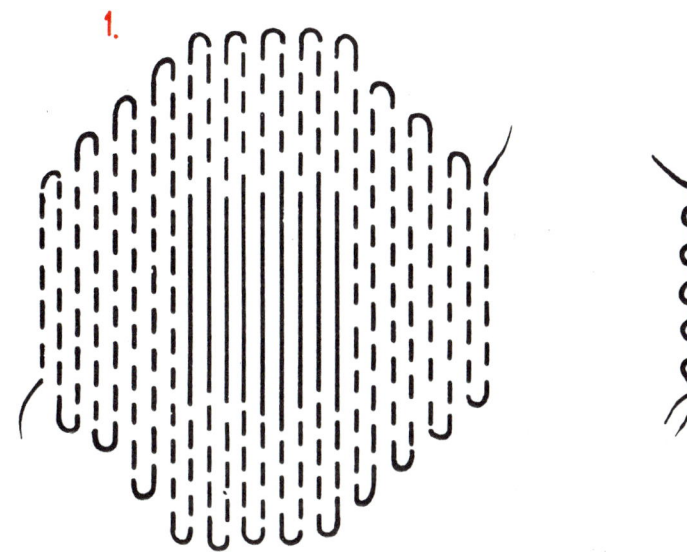

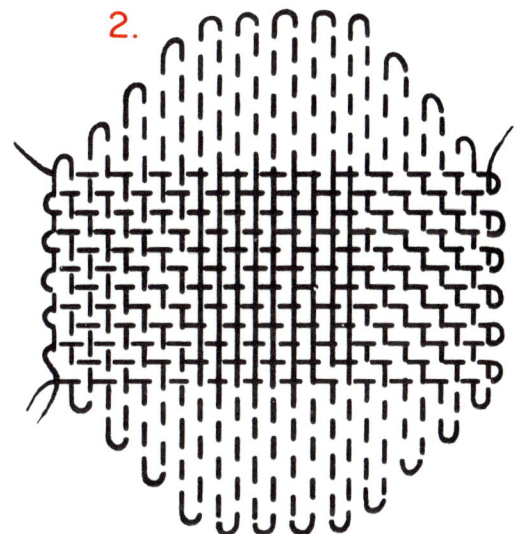

1. Trim edges in order to make a neat hole – a rectangle or square preferably

2. Working from the W.S., darn up and down, picking up all loose loops and following closely the finished shape of the darn which should be marked out with tacking thread.

3. Loops of thread should be left at the end of each row to allow for shrinkage.

4. Work across the darn so that double darning is worked over the hole and the area immediately surrounding it.

A DIAGONAL CUT DARN

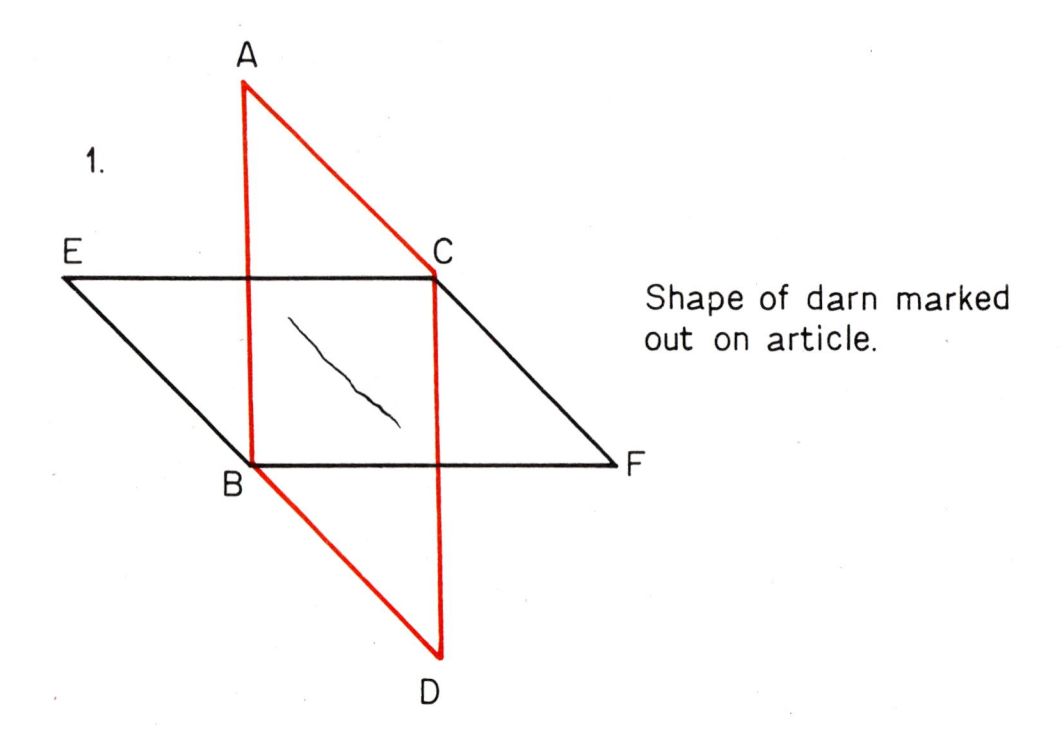

1.

Shape of darn marked out on article.

Fishbone raw edges together.
Start at A and work to B and following the shape to CD.
Restart at E and work to C and on to BF.

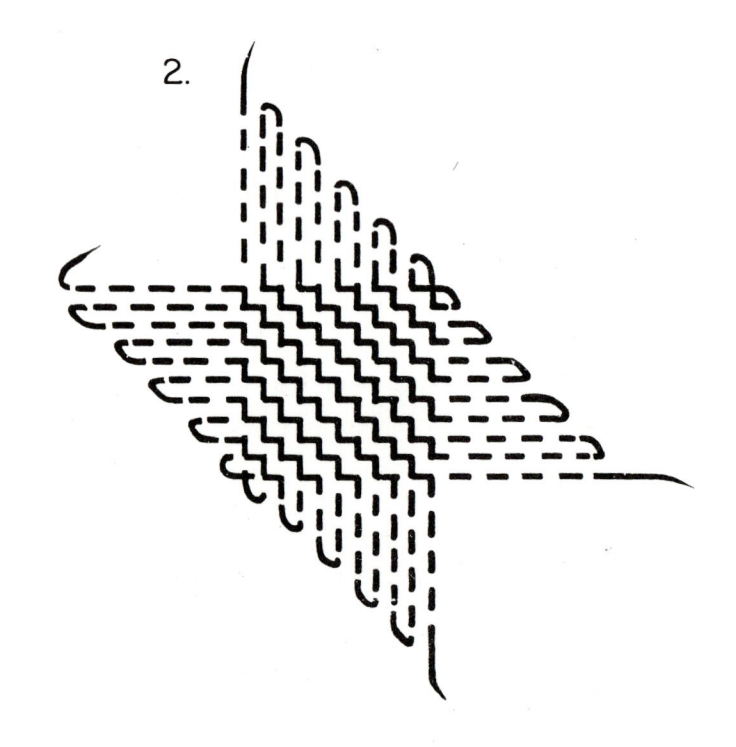

2.

HEDGE-TEAR DARN

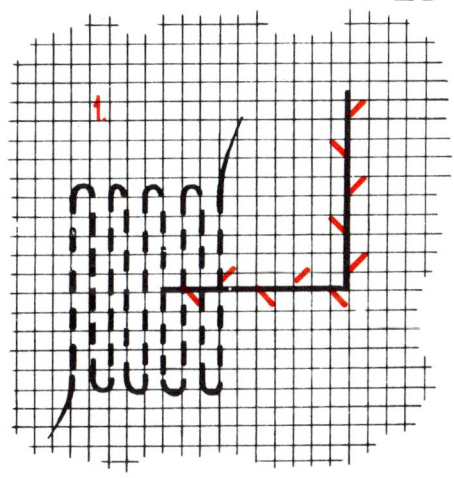

Raw edges fish-bone stitched together.

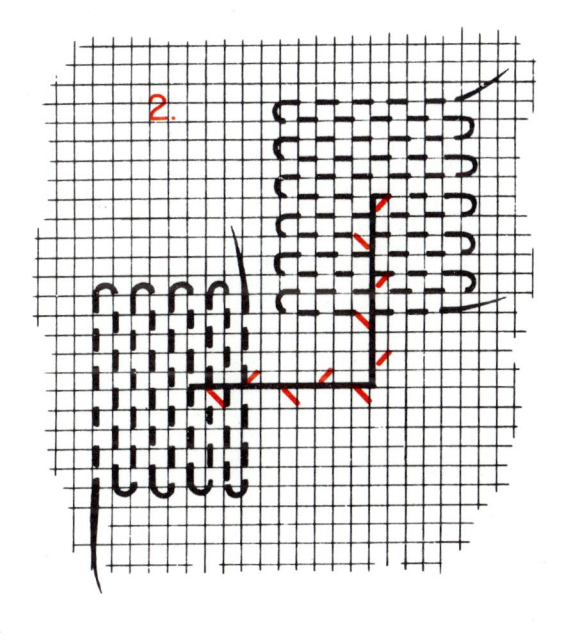

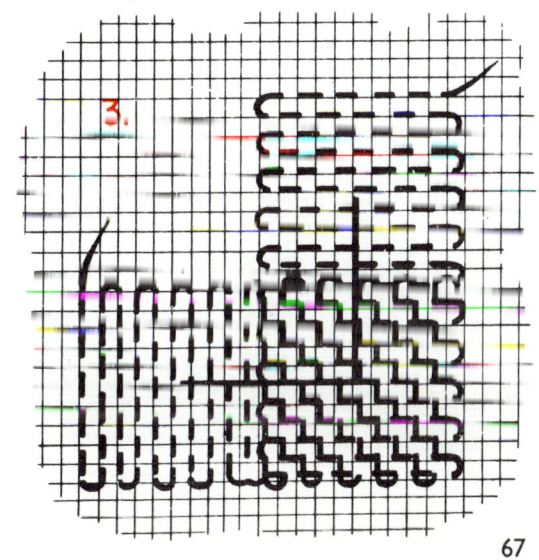

67

SWISS DARNING

<u>Uses</u>: 1. Darning a thin place on a hand knitted garment worked in stocking stitch
2. Working a design on a hand knitted garment — it is similar to Fair-Isle if worked on the R.S.

1. WORKING FROM RIGHT SIDE. (Plain knitting)

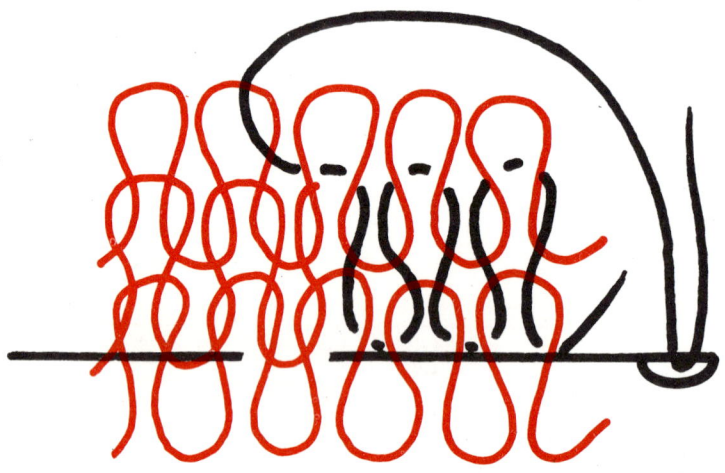

2. WORKING FROM WRONG SIDE. (Purl knitting)

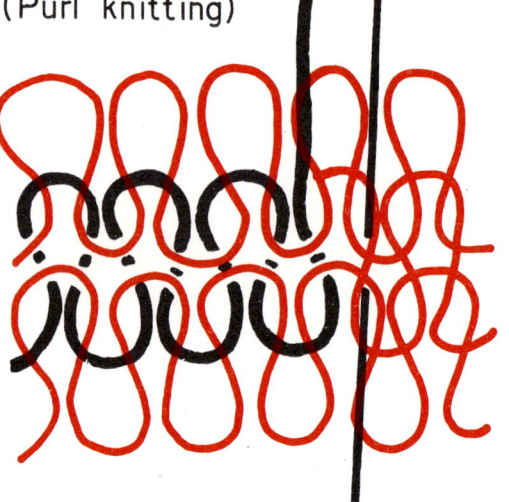

Points to remember.

1. Darning may be worked from right side or wrong side.
2. Wool should be a little finer than that used for knitting the garment.
3. Always place needle in centre of knitted loop.
4. Keep along same row of knitting.

MACHINE DARNING

Uses: a strong and quick method of repairing holes and strengthening thin places in household articles and underwear.

1. Follow instructions provided for the particular sewing machine being used. The presser foot may be removed altogether or a darning foot may replace the foot in general use. Also the feed should either be lowered or covered so that the teeth do not come into contact with the work. Movement is now free and the work must be guided carefully with the hands.
2. Use an embroidery frame so that the part to be darned is kept taut. Work backwards and forwards.
3. Use a fine thread and a fine needle.
4. Follow general rules for darning.
5. Patches may also be machine-darned in position on the W.S. by machining to a depth of $\frac{5}{8}''$ (1·5 cm) so that stitching lies $\frac{1}{8}''$ (·25 cm) beyond raw edges. The patch itself should be cut $\frac{3}{8}''$ (1 cm) larger than the hole on all sides.
6. A tear in household articles is best repaired by attaching a piece of tape underneath and machine-stitching closely in position.

Patching

General Rules:
1 The patch must be of the same material as the garment, or as near to it as possible in colour, texture, pattern and weave.
2 The patch must be large enough to cover the hole and also the thin part surrounding it.
3 The patch should be of a definite shape, e.g. square or rectangular, except when a patch has to be worked into a seam.
4 Selvedge threads should be matched with selvedge threads, weft with weft.
5 Patches on patterned material are placed on R.S. in order to match the design. This is also the case with garments worn next to the skin in order to make them more comfortable. All other patches are placed on the W.S.
6 The thread used should be suitable, taking special note of colour and texture.
7 All corners should be mitred except on woollen patches.

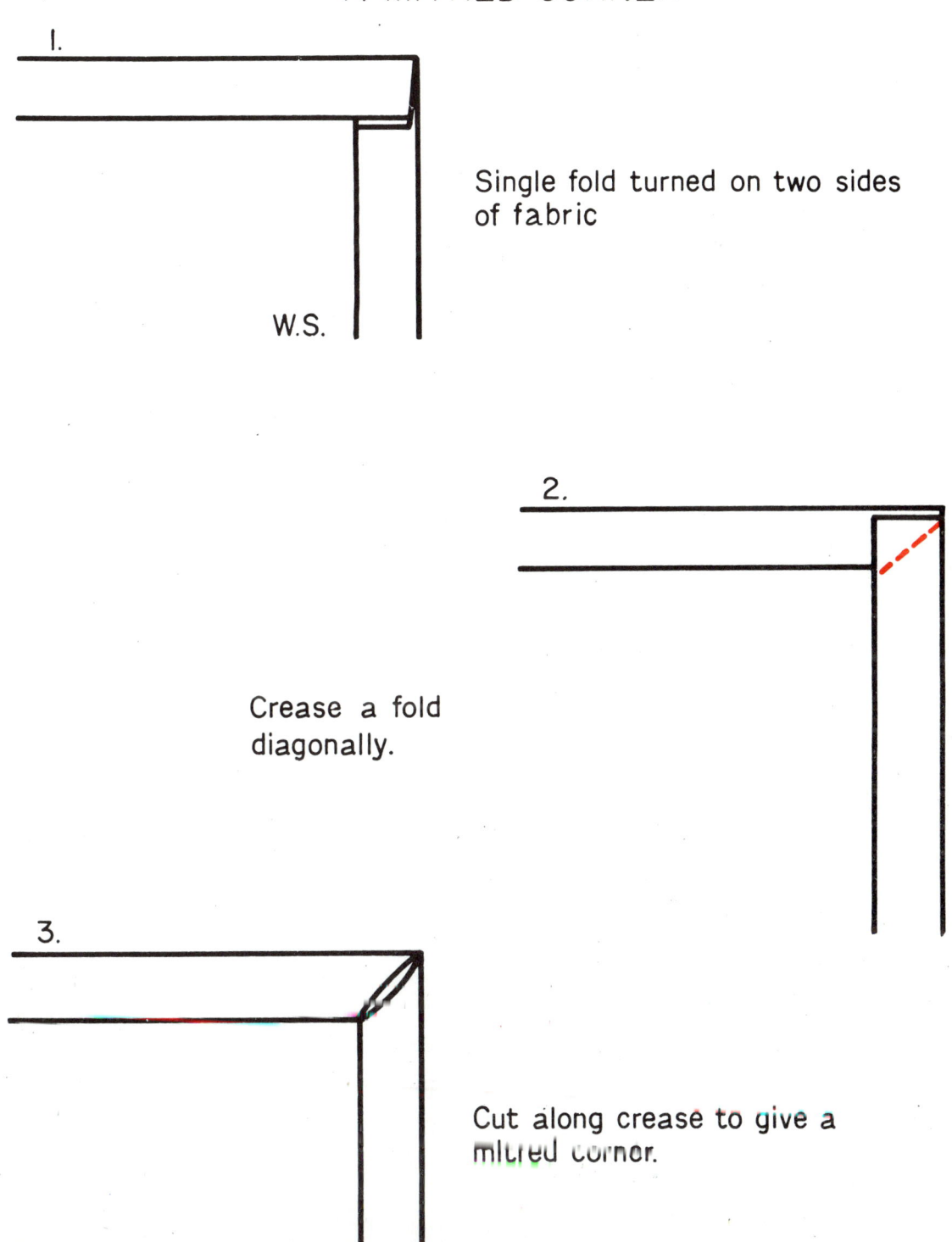

A MITRED CORNER

1.

Single fold turned on two sides of fabric

W.S.

2.

Crease a fold diagonally.

3.

Cut along crease to give a mitred corner.

A CALICO PATCH
(By hand)

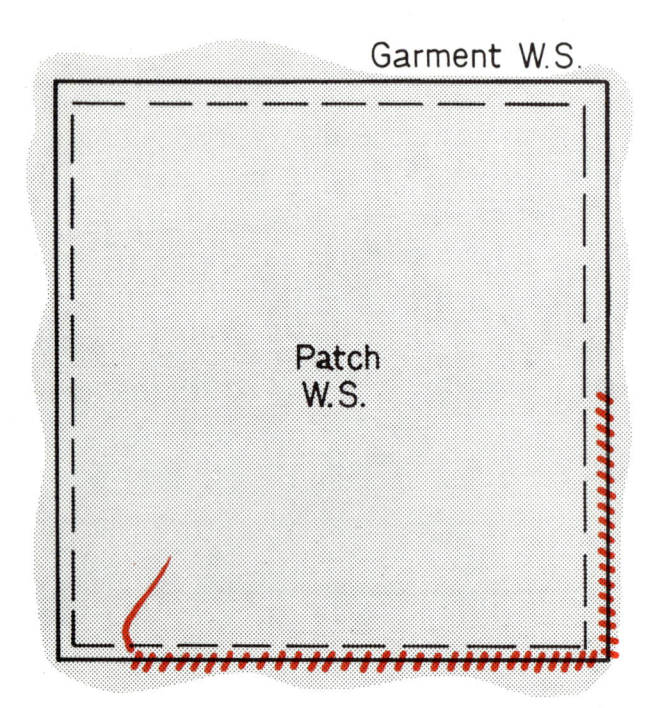

Garment W.S.

Patch W.S.

Hem patch on W.S.

Trim surplus fabric. Turn a fold on raw edges and hem in position on R.S.

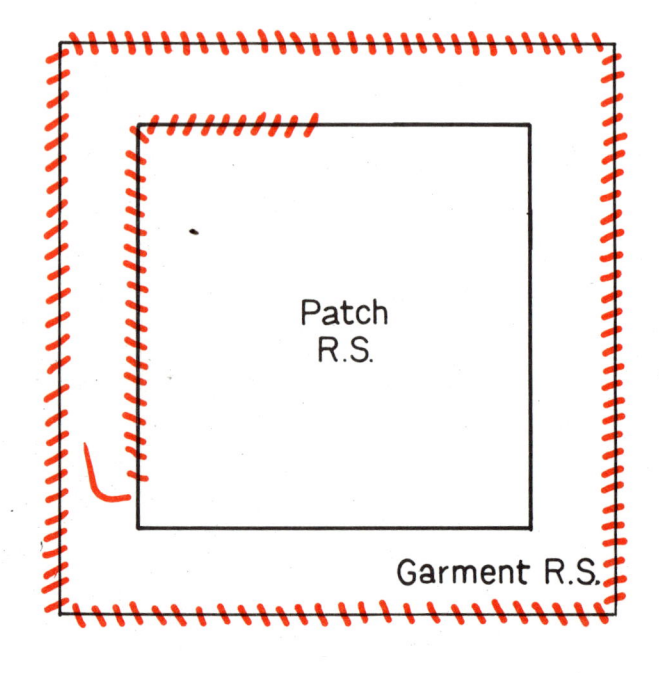

Patch R.S.

Garment R.S.

A CALICO PATCH
(By machine)

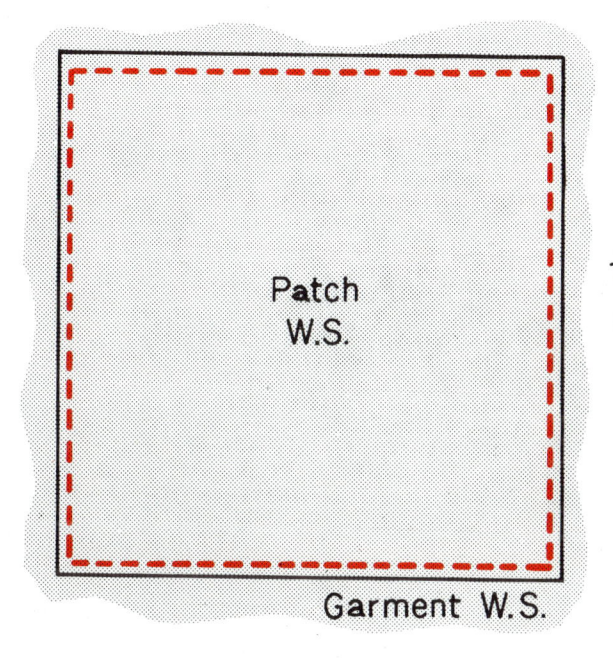

Tack and machine folded edge of patch.

Garment W.S.

2.

Trim away surplus fabric.
Turn a fold along edge.
Tack and machine.

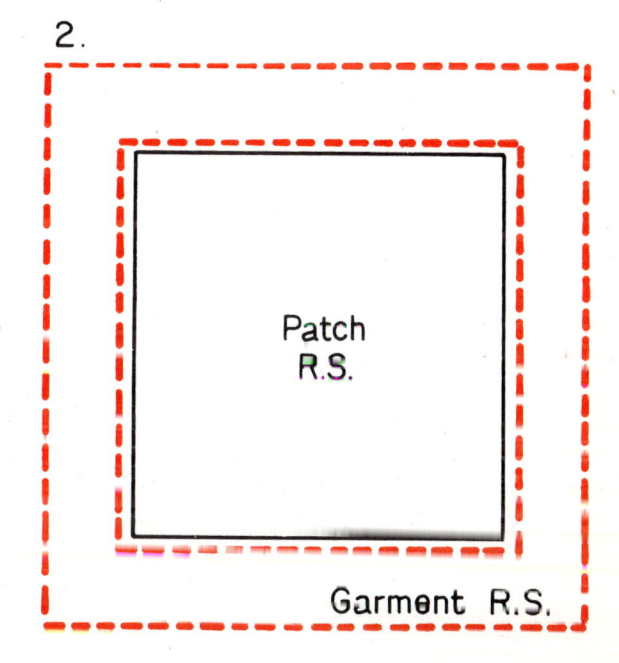

Garment R.S.

A WOOLLEN PATCH.

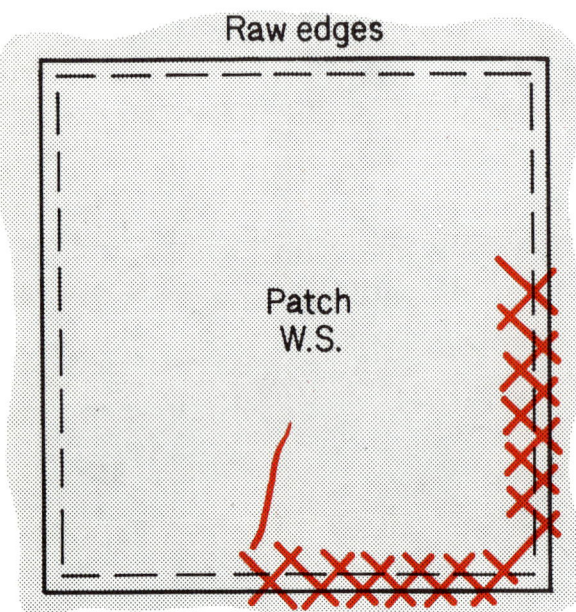

Patch W.S.

Garment W.S.

Raw edges

Herringbone stitch the raw edges in position on W.S.

Trim away surplus fabric herringbone stitch raw edges on R.S.

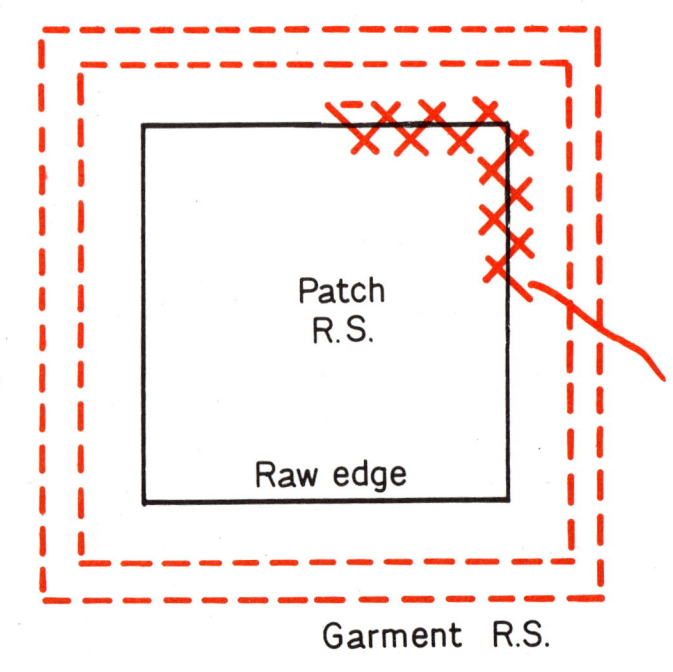

Patch R.S.

Raw edge

Garment R.S.

A PRINT PATCH

1.

Hem or oversew on R.S.

Patch R.S.

Garment R.S.

2.

Trim away surplus fabric. Blanket stitch raw edges on W.S

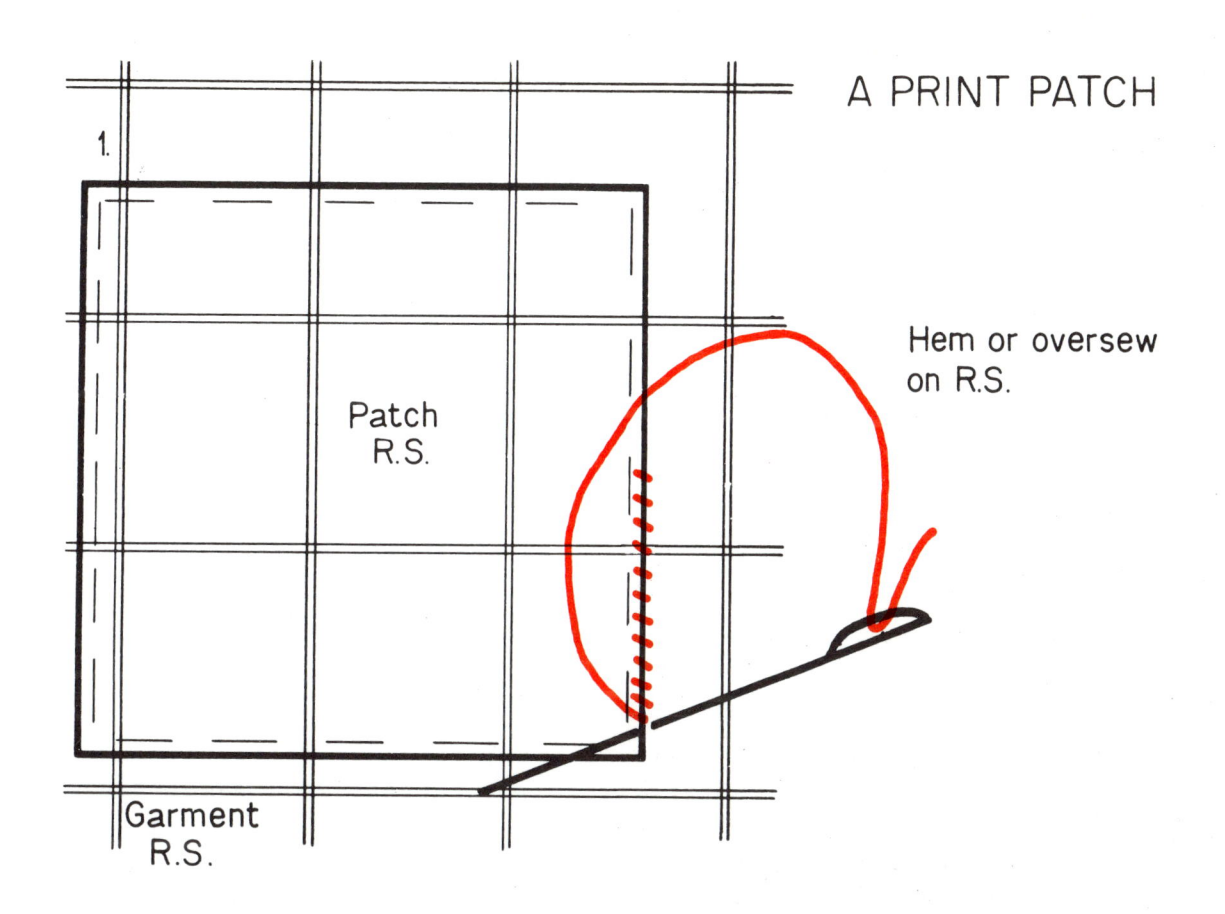

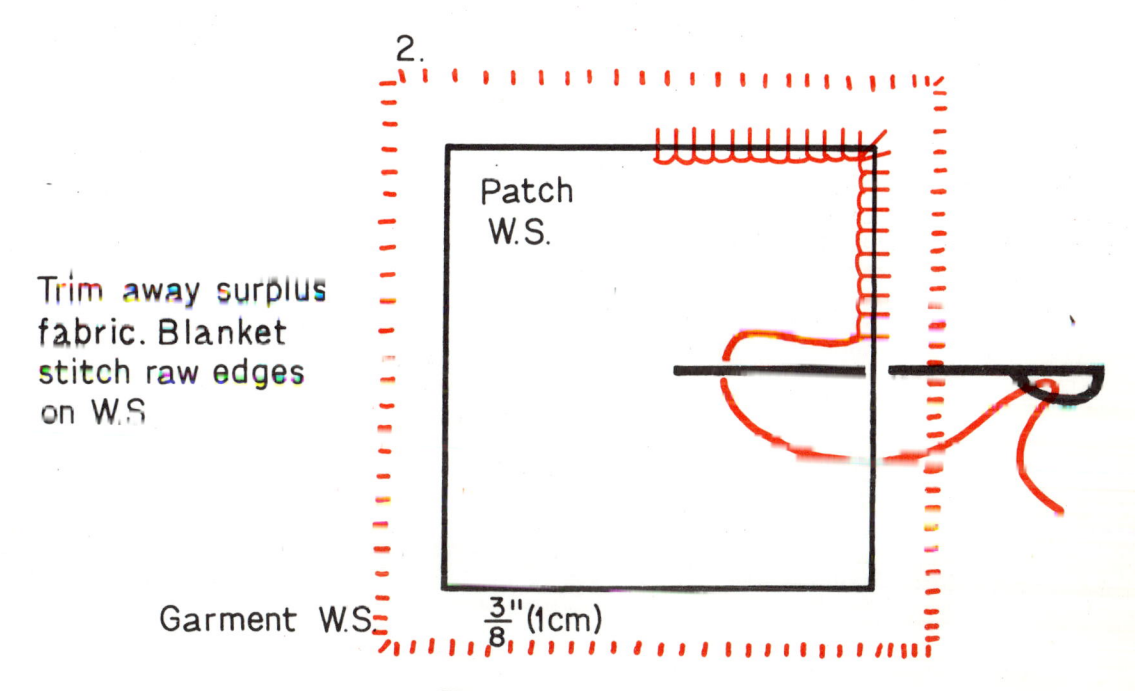

Patch W.S.

Garment W.S.

$\frac{3}{8}$" (1cm)

75

Fibres and Fabrics

Most fabrics are woven. Those which are non-woven include knitted fabrics, felt, lace, net, foam-backed fabrics and bonded fabrics.

All woven fabrics are made up of two sets of fibres or threads:
1 The selvedge threads (warp)
2 The weft threads (woof)

The selvedge threads are stretched on the rollers of the loom, while the weft thread is woven over and under, backwards and forwards, according to the type of weave chosen.

When cutting out, the selvedge threads, which are stronger than those of the weft, should take most of the strain, and therefore, as a general rule, they should run up and down the length of the garment.

Methods of distinguishing between selvedge (warp) and weft threads:
1 *By stretching the fabric*
   Weft threads stretch while the warp threads do not.
2 *By tearing the fabric*
   Short ends of threads appear where the warp threads are torn whereas the weft threads are longer and more irregular. The warp threads are more compact and highly twisted.
3 *By pulling the fabric sharply*
   The warp threads make a sharp sound whereas the weft threads make a dull sound.
4 *By examination of threads*
   There are more warp threads to a square inch of material than there are of weft threads.

Types of fibres:
1 Natural Fibres
   Animal fibres – wool, silk
   Vegetable fibres – cotton, linen

2 Man-made Fibres
   Rayons (viscose and acetate)
   Nylon
   Terylene
   Dacron
   Orlon
   Acrilan
   Courtelle, etc.

Animal fibres

WOOL

Source:
Sheep. Most of the world's supply of wool is produced in Australia, U.S.S.R., New Zealand, Argentina, South Africa. Most important manufacturers of woollen yarn – U.S.A., Britain, U.S.S.R., France, West Germany.

Various Fabrics available:
Felt, Flannel, Tweed, Knitted (Jersey), Bouclé, Velour, Gaberdine, Barathea, Worsted, Lightweight wool, Suitings, Serge, Blanket, Woolcrepe, etc.

Characteristics:
Warm. Absorbs well. Shrinks with harsh treatment. Ability to felt. Durable. Medium strength (weakest of the natural fibres). Great elasticity and is very resilient, thus making it easy to shed creases. Damaged by moths and perspiration. May be shaped with heat and pressure but scorches on direct application of dry heat.

Care:
1. Air and brush often. Protect from moths and perspiration.
2. Hand wash sweaters, underwear, socks, etc. in warm soapy water, squeezing gently and supporting weight of garment to avoid stretching. Do not soak, wring or rub. Dry immediately in a current of air.
3. If in doubt, dry clean woollen garments.
4. Press (not iron) on W.S. over a damp cloth and pressing cloth.
5. Air well.

Uses:
All types of wearing apparel, handbags, belts, braids, home furnishings, blankets, carpets, upholstery, drapes, knitting yarns.

Wool fibre under a microscope

Root   Tip

SILK

Source:
Silk-worms. Silk-producing countries – Japan, China, India, France, Mexico, etc.

Various Fabrics available:
Chiffon, Lace, Georgette, Satin, Taffeta, Tweed, Crepe de Chine, Velvet, Foulard, Net, Shantung (Wild Silk).

Characteristics:
Smooth and lustrous. Drapes well. Absorbent. Dyes and prints well. Durable, strong and fairly elastic. Lightweight and cool. (Denier is the weight in grammes of 9,000 metres of yarn. The finer the silk, the lower the denier.)

Care:
1. Lingerie and undergarments are always hand-washable, but garments labelled for dry-cleaning should always be dry-cleaned.
2. Wash by squeezing gently in warm soapy water, rinse, and roll in a towel before hanging to dry.
3. Iron on W.S. while still damp with a moderate iron. Iron Shantung and Tussore when bone dry.

Uses:
Wearing apparel including ties, scarves, gloves, hats, hosiery, shoes.
House furnishings, umbrellas, sewing thread.

Silk fibre under a microscope

Vegetable fibres

COTTON

Source:
Cotton plant which grows in tropical countries – Southern States of U.S.A., U.S.S.R., India, China, Egypt, Brazil, Pakistan, etc.

Various Fabrics available:
Calico, Poplin, Lawn, Gingham, Chintz, Drill, Denim, Lace, Cambric, Muslin, Net, Corduroy, Terry-towelling, Velveteen, Pique, Winceyette, Sateen, Seersucker, Glazed cotton, Flannelette.

Characteristics:
Very versatile. Easy to sew. Does not fray readily. Absorbs well. Strong (stronger when wet). Durable. Lightweight and cool. Dyes and bleaches easily. Resin finishes add crispness, repels water and resists creases. Resistant to moths and heat. Little elasticity. Flammable.

Care:
1. Cotton can stand very strong heat, and white cotton may be boiled.
2. Untreated cottons may be washed in hot water, by hand or machine.
3. Damp well before ironing on the W.S. with a hot iron. Some cottons, especially drip-dry and crease resistant, need little or no ironing.

Uses:
Summer dresses, skirts, blouses, shirts, hats, shoes, children's clothing, nightwear, sewing thread, overalls, house furnishings and many industrial uses.

Cotton fibre under a microscope

LINEN

Source:
Flax which is grown in large quantities in the U.S.S.R., France, the Netherlands, Belgium, Ireland.

Various Fabrics available:
Damask, Dress linen, Lace, Sheeting, Upholstery fabrics, Towelling, Crash, Handkerchief linen, etc.

Characteristics:
Very strong and durable (stronger than cotton). Absorbs very well – dyes and bleaches easily. Heavier in weight than cotton and frays more readily. Cool – a poor conductor of heat. It creases badly if not treated. It does not soil readily. It resists heat and insects. Prone to mildew if left damp for any length of time.

Care:
1 Machine or hand-washable. It can stand very strong heat and boiling.
2 It may be starched, though this is not always necessary with good linen.
3 Damp well before ironing with a hot iron on W.S. for a dull finish, or on R.S. for a shiny finish.

Uses:
Most outer clothing, handkerchiefs, petticoats, shoes, hats, handbags, house furnishings, table-cloths, tea towels, sheets, towels, table napkins, sewing thread, sails.

Linen fibre under a microscope

Man-made fibres

RAYON (VISCOSE)

Manufactured from cellulose which is treated with caustic soda and carbon bisulphide, the liquid then being forced into an acid bath thus causing cellulose to be regenerated.

Various Fabrics available:
Crepe, Jersey, Satin, Taffeta, Velvet, Net, Brocade, Moiré.

Characteristics:
Absorbs well – dyes easily (using a non-water based dye). Medium strength – much weaker when wet. Resembles silk in appearance – drapes well, yet it can also be produced to resemble linen, cotton or wool. Various finishes available – crease resistant, stain resistant, water repellent, etc. Flammable.

Care:
If washable, wash in warm soapy water, squeezing gently. Rinse thoroughly. Iron while still fairly damp with a cool iron. Brush and air frequently.

Uses:
Clothing – outerwear, underwear, nightwear, hats, handbags, shoes, furnishings, carpets, household articles, linings.

RAYON (ACETATE)

Manufactured by treating cellulose with acetic acid to form cellulose acetate. This is dissolved in acetone to form a liquid which is dry spun to form fibres.

Various Fabrics available:
Satin, Shirting, Suiting, Crepe, Knitted.

Characteristics:
Absorbs less water than viscose rayon and loses less strength when wet. Does not stain readily. Dries fairly quickly – keeps its shape when wet. Resists mildew. Does not burn readily. Softens and melts on application of dry heat.

Care:
1. If garment is washable, wash in warm soapy water. Rinse thoroughly. Do not squeeze or wring. Drip-dry in a current of air.
2. Iron with a cool iron on W.S. while the garment is very slightly damp.

Uses:
Dresses, evening gowns, blouses, underwear, nightwear, ties, shirts, pyjamas, rainwear, bathing suits.

NYLON

Nylon is known chemically as a polyamide – a group of synthetic fibres to which perlon and celon also belong.

Various Fabrics available:
Net, Satin, Taffeta, Velvet, Ribbon, Brushed nylon, Crepe, Damask.

Characteristics:
Durable. Very Strong. Very low absorption of moisture – does not stain easily, quick drying but is clammy to wear in hot weather. Resilient. High elasticity. Does not crease. Is not easily scratched. Resistant to moth and mildew. Melts on application of dry heat beyond 150°C. Turns yellow with excessive heat. Weakens with continuous exposure to light and air.

Care:
1. Wash often to retain whiteness.
2. Wash thoroughly in warm soapy water. Rinse well in warm water.
3. Drip dry for minimum creases.
4. If ironing is required, use a cool iron on W.S.

Uses:
Clothing, ribbon, lace, umbrellas, ropes, tyres, tarpaulins, sails.

ORLON etc.

Orlon, Acrilan and Courtelle belong to a group of synthetic fibres known chemically as polyacrylic.

Various Fabrics available:
Knitted fabrics, Shirting, Deep pile coating.

Characteristics:
Strong and durable. Excellent resistance to sunlight, weather and chemicals. Retains size and shape. Quick drying though not as clammy as some of the other synthetic fabrics. Softens and melts on application of dry heat above 150°C.

Care:
1. If garment is washable, squeeze gently in lukewarm soapy water. Remove excess water with a towel.
2. If ironing is necessary, use a cool iron on W.S. Heat-set pleats need only slight pressing after washing. Never use a damp cloth or steam iron.

Uses:
Pullovers, cardigans, underwear, overcoats, suits, dresses, furnishings.

TERYLENE

Terylene, as well as Dacron and Tetron, belong to a group of synthetic fibres known chemically as polyesters.

Various Fabrics available:
Suitings, Taffeta, knitted (Crimplene), Worsted, Linen, Flannel, etc. Also blended with other fibres.

Characteristics:
Very strong and durable. Resilient and elastic – crease resistant and keeps its shape. Extremely low absorption of water – dries very quickly – pleats retain their shape after washing. Is not easily scratched – withstands friction. Softens and melts on application of dry heat beyond 150°C.

Care:
If garment is washable, wash in warm soapy water by squeezing gently. Rinse thoroughly. Roll in a towel to remove excess water. If ironing is necessary, use a cool iron on W.S.

Uses:
Clothing, sewing thread, upholstery, ropes, industrial uses, car seat covers.

DYNEL

Dynel and Rhovyl belong to a class of synthetic fibres known chemically as polyvinyl chlorides.

Various Fabrics available:
Jersey, Twill, Flannel, Glove fabrics, Damask, Bathing-suit fabrics, Deep pile coatings, Fur-imitations.

Characteristics:
Very strong and durable. Very resilient and elastic – does not crease. Resistant to insects, mildew and chemicals – does not stain easily. Softens and melts on application of dry heat – can be moulded into various shapes.

Care:
If garment is washable, wash in warm soapy water. Rinse thoroughly. Dry in a current of air. Iron with a cool iron, protecting the fabric with a dry cloth.

Uses:
Hats, Bathing suits, Coats, Dresses, Socks, Nightwear, Toys, Children's clothing.

Fabric blends and mixtures

Different fibres are very often blended or mixed together to produce new fabrics. Blending takes place at the fibre stage whereas the mixing process is carried out at the weaving (or knitting) stage of the fabric.

One man-made fibre may be used with another, natural fibres are used together, and there are very successful blends and mixtures of natural fibres with a man-made fibre. Each fibre retains its own characteristics and the fabric produced, therefore, must be treated accordingly.

Fibres are blended or mixed together for the following reasons:

1 To produce a cheaper fabric

   Examples: Cotton/linen, Cotton/wool, rayon/cotton, rayon/wool.

2 To produce a fabric where one fibre is used to minimise the shortcomings of another

   Examples: Terylene/linen: Terylene reduces drying time and helps to shed creases.
   Cotton/wool: cotton reduces bulk and counteracts the possibility of shrinkage.

3 To produce a fabric where one fibre complements the other.

   Examples: Wool/nylon, which gives a warm, hardwearing fabric. Wool/terylene: wool provides warmth, whereas terylene prevents the fabric from creasing, allows pleats to be permanently set and enables the fabric to be washed without fear of shrinkage.
   Cotton/Terylene: this results in a crisp crease-resisting, quick-drying, non-iron, durable, attractive, absorbent and therefore comfortable fabric, suitable for making blouses, shirts, dresses and lingerie.

Identification of fibres

Fabrics may be identified in the following ways:
1 By reading labels provided on fabrics and garments.
2 Appearance and feel of fabric, though it must be remembered that one fibre is often made to appear like another.
3 Microscopic appearance of fibres.
4 Simple tests:

FABRIC	Fibre held in a flame and then withdrawn	Nature of Fumes	Nature of Ash	Other simple tests
WOOL	Smoulders. Does not flare up.	Alkaline fumes. Strong smell of burnt feathers.	Formation of a black bead.	Dissolves in 5% solution hot caustic soda.
SILK	Smoulders.	Alkaline fumes. Smell of burnt feathers.	Formation of a black bead.	Dissolves in 5% solution hot caustic soda.
COTTON	Flares up with a yellow flame.	Acid fumes. Smell of burnt paper.	Very little grey ash.	Dissolves in concentrated solution sulphuric acid.
LINEN	Flares up with yellow flame.	Acid fumes. Smell of burnt paper.	Grey ash.	Dissolves in concentrated solution sulphuric acid.
RAYON VISCOSE	Flares up.	Acid fumes. Smell of burnt paper.	Grey ash.	Considerable loss of strength when wet.
RAYON ACETATE	Flares up.	Acid fumes. Acid smell.	Formation of a black bead.	Dissolves in acetone.
NYLON	Melts. Shrinks away from flame.	White smoke.	Hard grey bead.	—
ORLON	Burns and melts.	Aromatic smell.	Hard black bead.	—
TERYLENE	Melts and shrinks. Will burn eventually with a yellow flame.	Sooty smoke. Aromatic smell.	Hard bead.	—
DYNEL	Melts and shrivels away from flame.	—	Formation of black bead.	Dissolves in acetone.

With fibre mixtures, all tests must be applied until the fibres are singled out and identified.

Interlining

Interlinings, such as Vilene and Lantor, which are available in the shops nowadays, are made from a mixture of natural and man-made fibres bonded together chemically, or by means of an adhesive or with the use of heat.

Uses:

For strengthening, stiffening, giving body or giving shape to certain parts of a garment, thus giving the garment a crisp and better finish.

Suitable for:

Collars, cuffs, waistbands, belts, lapels, pockets, facings, ensuring a permanent knife-edge to pleats, backing buttonholes, especially if the material frays, making stiff underskirts, eliminating the necessity of using bones in strapless bodices.

Points to remember about interlining:

1 It may be washed or dry-cleaned.
2 It is shrink-resistant and crease-resistant.
3 **Non-woven interlining does not fray and may therefore be cut in any direction.**
4 There is no bias as such, and it does not stretch. It is, therefore, not suitable for use on parts of a garment, such as coat collars, which have to be stretched and shaped.
5 It is available in a wide range of grades. It should be bought according to the weight and texture of the fabric with which it is to be used – the lighter and softer the material, the lighter the interlining to be used.
6 One grade which is most useful for general use is adhesive backed and may be stuck permanently on to the W.S. of a garment by pressing with a warm iron. This is most suitable for small areas.
7 To avoid bulky seams, cut the interlining slightly smaller than the actual pattern. Iron-on interlinings may be cut with the seam-line as it is stuck rather than stitched in position.

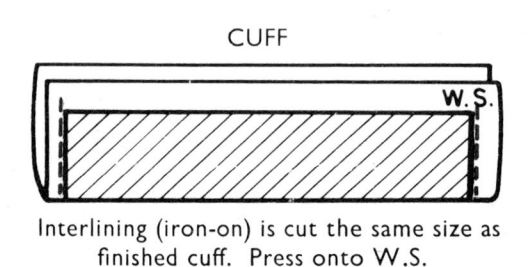

CUFF

W.S.

Interlining (iron-on) is cut the same size as finished cuff. Press onto W.S.

Hints on how to handle difficult fabrics

Velvet and Corduroy:
1 Choose a simple style – beginners are advised to avoid buttonholes and pleats.
2 Buy sufficient fabric as all pattern pieces must be cut out in the same direction.
3 The pile should run upwards towards neckline. This gives a richer colour and better wear.
4 Use good quality pins and pin only within seam allowance in case you leave a mark on the velvet.
5 Tack carefully and machine stitch without much pressure, using 11–12 stitches per inch.
6 Some of the new velvets may be pressed lightly on W.S. but this is not always the case. Generally it is safer to hold the garment taut between two persons and steam open the seams. Do not over-handle the velvet, especially when damp.
7 Finish off all raw edges by hand or with a machined edge-stitch.

Lace:
1 Choose a design that is not too complicated. Beginners should avoid buttonholes and any difficult processes of construction.
2 Although lace may be worn over a slip, it is advisable to underline very sheer lace – this strengthens it and also makes it easier to get neat and inconspicuous seams. The lace and lining pieces must be tacked firmly together and then regarded as a single fabric. Hems should be stitched to the underlining.
3 When no underlining is used, lace should be stitched along seam-line and again between seam-line and edge. Trim away to the 1st line of machine-stitching and overcast edge if necessary.
4 When it is necessary to match the pattern on the lace, overlap two pieces so that the pattern matches exactly. Tack and whip-stitch the two pieces together following the lines of the lace pattern. Repeat on underside. Trim away surplus lace.
5 Neaten necklines and armholes with strips of fabric cut on the cross – as a binding or facing (if lined).
6 It is necessary to loosen the tension of the thread when machining, and sometimes to use a piece of tissue paper underneath the fabric. This avoids puckering and prevents the lace from getting caught in the feed.

7 Press on W.S., the heat of the iron depending on the yarn used for making the lace.

Plastic (P.V.C. or Vinyl):

1 Choose a simple style with very little detail. Beginners are advised to choose raglan sleeves rather than set-in-sleeves, which require careful manipulation.
2 Pins leave a permanent mark and, therefore, must not be used. The paper pattern may be kept in place by means of weights or tapes.
3 Use chalk for marking, and paper clips for holding two pieces of fabric together.
4 Machine-stitch very carefully, using 8–12 stitches per inch. Tissue paper may be used underneath to avoid fabric being caught up by the teeth.
5 Use flat-stitched or open seams. Tape and bias-binding may be used for strengthening seams and neatening edges. Buttonholes should be worked by hand, and zips, hooks or snap fasteners may be used for openings.
6 Do not press as it will melt on application of dry heat.
7 It cannot be laundered or dry-cleaned, but it may be wiped with a damp cloth or sponged.

Courtelle Jersey:

1 Choose a simple style.
2 Adjust the pattern to fit the figure before cutting out.
3 Tack and fit carefully so that it is not necessary to unpick a seam.
4 Use medium sized zig-zag machine-stitch with a speed which is not too fast. Stretch the seam slightly as it is being sewn – this gives a better finish. When seams are on the cross, stitch a tape along seam line.
5 Neaten raw edges with overcasting or a machined edge-stitch.
6 Never use a damp cloth or steam iron. Press on W.S. with a dry cool iron.

Fur Fabrics:

Fur fabric is available by the yard and may be used successfully by the home dressmaker.

1 Select a simple pattern with very little detail.
2 Patterns may be cut crosswise or lengthwise, but all pieces must be cut in the same direction.
3 Fur may be pinned but use a razor blade for cutting so that the hairs are not damaged.

4 Stitch with a large machine-stitch. Seams may be unpicked and re-stitched as fur disguises any flaws. Using a pin, pull hairs out of the seam to give an even surface.
5 Press with a warm dry iron.
6 Line to the edge of garment as facings made of fur are bulky. Stitch tape to hemline, turn to W.S. and handstitch in position.
7 Use up bits of fur which are left over for making collars, handbags, muffs, cushions etc.

General rules for pressing

'Press as you sew' is one of the basic rules of dressmaking.
Ironing is a free movement of the iron.
Pressing is pressure on one spot, no movement, but the lifting and pressing of the iron.

Equipment:

Iron: It should not be too light especially for pressing thick materials. An iron which is thermostatically controlled is especially useful because it can be regulated for the requirements of any fabric. A steam iron permits pressing without a damp pressing cloth.

Ironing Board: This should be protected with a padding and covered with calico which can be removed for washing. An asbestos square should be available for standing the iron. It should be possible to adjust the height of the board according to the working height of user.

Sleeve Board: A sleeve board is especially useful for pressing short seams and sleeves. A small pad may be made for use on curved seams, darts and any small areas.

Pressing Cloth: A pressing cloth is necessary to protect fabrics from the direct heat of the iron. Also, a damp piece of muslin is especially useful when a steam iron is not available.

General Rules:
1. All equipment should be kept in good condition.
2. If the iron is not automatically controlled, it should be carefully tested for heat as it is essential that the correct heat be used for different fabrics:

Wool: Press on W.S. with a fairly hot iron over a damp muslin and pressing cloth.
Silk: Iron on W.S. when still damp with a moderate iron. Shantung should be bone dry.
Cotton may be ironed on R.S. or W.S. while still slightly damp.
Linen: Damp well before ironing with a hot iron on R.S. (for a shiny finish), or on W.S. (for a dull finish).
Rayon: Iron at low heat while still fairly damp.
Nylon: If ironing is required, use a cool iron when fabric is dry.
Courtelle: Press on W.S. with a cool iron when bone dry. Never use a damp cloth or steam iron.
Crimplene: Needs no ironing except during construction when pressing is very important.
Velvet and Corduroy: All seams must be steamed and *not* pressed.

3. Never rest the iron on the fabric – keep it moving constantly to avoid marking.
4. Always iron with the straight grain on single fabric, and smooth the material into correct shape so that fabric is not stretched or creased. If a garment is cut on the true bias, care must be taken not to stretch it while pressing.
5. All darts and tucks should be pressed towards the sides or centre back. On all heavy fabrics, cut all darts and press open.
6. Work the point of the iron into all gathers – do not press them flat.
7. Never press in folds in bed linen, centre of sleeves or C.B. of blouses.
8. Lace and embroidery should be ironed or pressed on the W.S. over a towel to avoid flattening of pattern.
9. The lower edge of a hem may be well pressed to give a firm, true hem-line. All tacking should be removed before the final pressing.
10. All seams should be pressed before being crossed by another seam. The seam allowance at the waist may be pressed up or down according to the style of the garment.
11. Do not over-press.
12. All garments should be well aired before hanging them carefully in a wardrobe or folding and laying them in a drawer.

Stain removal

General Rules:
1 Whenever possible, stains should be removed while still fresh.
2 The garment should be washed if it is washable, but the water used should not be too hot as this may set the stain.
3 If chemicals are to be used, try a little out on a scrap of fabric or on the inside of the garment, in case it removes the dye as well as the stain.
4 When using chemicals or solvents, always work from outside the stain and avoid making a ring. A pad should be held underneath so that the stain may be transferred onto it from the garment.
5 Some solvents used are highly inflammable and others are poisonous, therefore great care must be taken in their storage.
6 Stains on garments needing dry cleaning should be marked on the garment and the cleaners told what has caused the stain.

Special Problems:
1 *Scorch Marks:* There is no treatment for bad scorching as this would have damaged the fibres. For slight marks, soak in glycerine or sponge with a solution of borax and water ($\frac{1}{2}$ oz. borax to $\frac{1}{2}$ pint water). Launder.
2 *Tar:* Remove as much tar as possible, then rub immediately with carbon tetrachloride or turpentine. Launder.
3 *Perspiration:* Sponge with a solution of vinegar and water (1 tablespoonful to 1 pint), or with a solution of one part ammonia to nine parts water. If odour persists, soak garment in a solution of 1 tablespoon borax to 1 pint water. Launder.
4 *Lipstick:* Wash in warm soapy water. If necessary, soften the stain with glycerine, then wash.
5 *Mildew:* Old stains are difficult to remove and actually rot the fabric. Apply a little lemon juice, leaving the fabric to dry in the sun. A little bleach may be applied to white articles.
6 *Mud:* Allow the stain to dry completely. Brush off the caked mud. Launder.
7 *Egg:* Soak in cold salted water – 1 teaspoon to 1 pint.
8 *Blood:* Wash in cool soapy water.
9 *Ball Point Pen:* Dab the stain with methylated spirit. Wash in warm soapy water.
10 *Hair Lacquer:* Dab stain with methylated spirit or amyl acetate. Launder.
11 *Rust:* Sprinkle white articles with salts of lemon, rubbing it in with a bone spoon. Pour boiling water through the stain.

12 *Grass:* Treat with methylated spirits. Launder.
13 *Tea:* Sponge with a warm solution of borax and water (1 oz. to 1 pint). Rinse.
14 *Fruit Juice:* Soak in cold water. Wash in solution of borax and water (1 oz. to 1 pint) and launder. If stain is set, soften with glycerine and then launder.